Anna Johnson

Education by Doing

Or, occupations and busy work, for primary classes

Anna Johnson

Education by Doing
Or, occupations and busy work, for primary classes

ISBN/EAN: 9783337426149

Printed in Europe, USA, Canada, Australia, Japan

Cover: Foto ©Paul-Georg Meister /pixelio.de

More available books at **www.hansebooks.com**

EDUCATION BY DOING

OR

OCCUPATIONS AND BUSY WORK, FOR PRIMARY CLASSES

By ANNA JOHNSON

Teacher in the Children's Aid Society Schools, New York City

WITH A PREFATORY NOTE BY EDWARD R. SHAW, PRINCIPAL OF
THE YONKERS (N. Y.) HIGH SCHOOL

"It is not the intention of sportive instruction that the child should be spared effort, or delivered from it; but that thereby a passion should be wakened in him, which shall both necessitate and facilitate the strongest exertion."—JEAN PAUL

NEW YORK
E. L. KELLOGG & CO.

COPYRIGHT, 1884, BY
E. L. KELLOGG & CO., NEW YORK.

Prefatory.

In observing the results achieved by the Kindergarten, educators have felt that Frœbel's great discovery of education by occupations must have something for the public school—that a further application of "the putting of experience and action in the place of books and abstract thinking," could be made beyond the fifth or sixth year of the child's life. This book is an outgrowth of this idea, conceived in the spirit of the New Education.

It will be widely welcomed, we believe, as it gives concrete methods of work—the very aids primary teachers are in search of. There has been a wide discussion of the subject of education, and there exists no little confusion in the mind of many a teacher as to how he should improve upon methods that have been condemned. There is a general desire and demand for better methods. The principles enunciated by Spencer "that science is evolved out of its corresponding art," and "that the abstract is to be reached by way of the concrete," are as true in their applications with reference to teachers as to pupils. And therefore, whoever gives concrete methods, based upon right principles, is doing the most to aid the great body of teachers, and is laying the surest foundation for a recognition of the principles of the science of education.

It is not to be supposed that all primary schools can use the entire range of occupations here given and suggested. Each can, however, find a great deal to weave into its plan of work, to give variety, interest, and spirit, and to counteract that tendency toward dull drill—the pitfall of so many schools.

Many of the exercises will, perhaps, have to be divided, as children should be carried no faster than they can fully comprehend; being careful always to remember the great principle that the object of concrete work is to aid the child in abstracting, and that only after many repetitions is he able to do this. When he has abstracted, he is at that moment ready to pass to new work. The years stated at the head of most of the chapters, have in view the average school. No doubt many schools will find that much can be used earlier, while others will use the same matter later, according to the grading of their work.

"Busy-work" has now become a necessity in all primary teaching. Teachers who have not had opportunity to visit those schools whence busy-work took its form and name, nor to attend the few normal schools that make it an adjunct of their methods in primary work, will find the chapters devoted to that subject especially valuable; and not only so in direction but also in suggestiveness.

Throughout the entire book the evident skill of the author as a teacher clearly manifests itself, and the spirit and enthusiasm which prompted these pages cannot fail to be imparted thereby to others.

EDWARD R. SHAW.

Yonkers, N. Y.

Contents.

	PAGE
INTRODUCTION,	9

ARITHMETIC.

Exercises with Blocks to teach Number,	13
Exercises with Beans to teach Number,	15
Exercises with Cards to teach Roman Number,	17
Exercises with Sticks to teach Roman Number,	19
Exercises with Pins to teach Number,	19
Exercises with Shoe Pegs to teach Number,	20
Exercises with Flags to teach Number,	24
Exercises with Sticks to teach Numeration,	25
Exercises with Toy Money to teach Subtraction,	28
Exercises with Toy Money to teach Division,	29
Exercises with Toy Money to teach the Value of Real Money,	31
Exercises with Cards to teach Mental Arithmetic,	33

WEIGHTS AND MEASURES.

	PAGE
Exercises with Clock Dials,	40
Exercises with Rules to teach Long Measure,	42
Exercises with Weights to teach Avoirdupois Weight,	45
Exercises with Measures to teach Liquid Measure,	46

FORM AND GEOGRAPHY.

Exercises with Blocks to teach Position,	48
Exercises with Shoe Pegs to teach Form,	50
Exercises with Pins to teach Form,	51
Exercises with Sticks to teach Position of Lines,	53
Exercises with Sticks to teach Angles,	54
Exercises with Wire to teach Curved Lines,	56
Exercises with Objects to teach Surfaces,	57
Exercises with Clay to teach Form,	59
Exercises with Sticks to teach Plane Figures,	60
Exercises with Paper to teach Form,	62
Exercises with Shoe Pegs in teaching Form and Number,	63
Exercises with Blocks in teaching Solid Figures,	64
Exercises with the Moulding-board to teach Geography,	66
Exercises with Flags in teaching Geography,	74

COLOR AND FORM.

Exercises with Gelatine Papers to teach Color,	76
Exercises with Worsted to teach Color,	79
Exercises with Flags to teach Color,	79
Exercises with Shoe Pegs to teach Color,	81
Exercises with Flags to teach Form and Color,	81

LANGUAGE.

Exercises with Pictures to teach Language,	82
Exercises with Cards to teach Language,	83

BUSY WORK.

	PAGE
Busy-work to aid in Reading, Writing and Spelling,	84
Busy-work in Language to teach Correct Use of Verb,	84
Busy-work in Language to teach Correct Use of Article,	86
Busy-work, Omitted Words,	87
Busy-work, Opposites,	88
Busy-work, Comparisons,	90
Busy-work, Definitions,	91
Busy-work, Preferences,	92
Busy-work in Drawing,	93
Busy-work in Drawing and Coloring,	94
Busy-work, Questions,	95

MISCELLANEOUS.

Occupations—Exercises with Card-board, Paper, etc.,	95
Slat-Weaving,	98
Exercises with Scrap-Books,	98
Exercises in Sewing,	99
Exercises with Paper in Making Flowers,	100

SLATE WORK.

Slate Work,	101
Slate Work, Miscellaneous,	103
Exercises with Objects to teach the Kingdoms,	104
Exercises with Objects to teach the terms, Natural and Manufactured,	106
Exercises with Occupation Cards to Teach Language and Number,	107

Introduction.

It is the purpose of this little book to show some of the many ways, and suggest others, in which young children may be kept pleasantly and profitably employed in schools and families.

How to keep little ones happy, busy and orderly, has been a problem hard to solve. Happy, because childhood should be the embodiment of happiness; busy, because little fingers and bodies were made to be busy; and orderly, because order is essential to progress.

It is the part of wisdom to direct, not to suppress, the activities of nature. Children, if well and strong, are full of animal life. How shall we use this life to advance education ? When left to themselves they are continually seeking occupation; their vivid imaginations give life to everything.

People have come to acknowledge that the methods nature adopts must be the best. A Being of Infinite wisdom and love cannot err in His plans.

The Kindergarten acknowledges this principle, and very beautifully provides for it. It is an elaborate system, requires special training, is expensive, and demands an increased force of teachers; and is therefore impracticable in ungraded schools, or in large classes. But cannot an approximation to the Kindergarten be attained in our schools?

Children must be taught, not only to see, but to use all their senses; to bring in a store of knowledge through all the outer channels. They need to make, select, and combine for and by themselves, really to learn and retain the knowledge gained.

Constant repetition is also necessary in primary teaching, but this often leads to monotony. In order to keep up the interest and have the old story fresh and attractive, it is necessary to change its clothing often.

For these reasons, it is not only expedient to introduce as great a variety of objects in primary teaching as possible, but also to use as great a variety as possible in teaching one truth. Sticks, blocks, beans, papers, wires, shoe-pegs, pictures, sand, and many other inexpensive objects are easily obtained in large quantities, and may be put to good use in teaching by using them in a systematic, instructive and orderly way.

It is an acknowledged fact that children who enter business young, become very expert in whatever department they are placed. They are sharp, quick, and know much more practically than those who have attended school much longer and are better versed in book knowledge. Why is this? Is it not because they acquire immediately, practical, instead of theoretical knowledge?

Our schools, therefore, will fit the children for their future life, in the degree that they become practical.

Let the children handle, do, think, and find out for themselves in every conceivable way, for that is the way their knowledge in infancy is gained, so let it continue on the same plain as far as possible.

The following lessons show how all the children may be employed at the same time, both under the direction of the teacher, and by themselves.

It is hoped they may meet with favor and be of service in primary work.

EDUCATION BY DOING.

EXERCISES WITH BLOCKS TO TEACH NUMBER.
FOR CHILDREN IN FIRST YEAR AT SCHOOL.

Give each child a bag of small blocks. Tell each one to take out one block and place it on the desk. Ask different ones to tell what they have done. Have them point out one of several objects, naming the object each time. The teacher may then place the figure 1 upon the board and tell them that is called one.

Tell them to take out one more block and place beside the other. Ask how many blocks they have now. Ask what make two. Have them repeat, "One block and one block make two blocks." Have them hold up one finger on each hand, then place them together and repeat, "One finger and one finger make two fingers." Have them find two of a variety of things. Have them go to the board and make two marks, two crosses, two dots; let them clap, shake hands, shake or nod the head two times. Then place the figure 2 on the board and tell them its meaning.

Proceed with the other numbers in a similar manner. The greatest variety is essential in order to keep up the interest and to be sure the children are thorough.

Have them count forward and backward together and separately.

Have them place a certain number of blocks and then take away one and state how many are left, and how they obtained it. In this way let subtraction go hand in hand with addition.

To test them as to the value of figures, the teacher may make a figure on the board, and call upon some one to make as many marks as that figure means, another to make as many dots, another to hold up as many fingers. Let the class decide who are right.

The teacher may tell a simple story in which small numbers are to be continually added and subtracted; letting the children give the results each time; as, "Johnny had one penny in one pocket and one in another,—his uncle came to see him and gave him one more,—he went to the store and spent one,—on his way home he lost one,—he earned two by doing an errand,—etc."

At each pause let the children raise their hands. Call upon different ones each time for the answer.

As soon as possible have the children relate the stories, the class answering as before.

EXERCISES WITH BEANS TO TEACH NUMBER.

FOR CHILDREN IN FIRST YEAR.

Give the children bags of beans. Ask them to place one bean on the desk. How many beans must you place with it to make two? Have them recite, "One and one make two." Ask what may be written on the board. The teacher may write $1 + 1 = 2$.

The signs used should be previously explained, so the children will be perfectly familiar with them.

Who can give an example using these numbers?

Make it four beans. How did you do it? What must be written on the board? Who can give an example?

Recite, "Two and two make four."

Make it three. What did you do? What must be written on the board? What sign must be used now? Why? Give an example. Recite,—"One from four leaves three."

Make it six. How did you do it? What must be written on the board? Give an example. Recite,—"Three and three make six."

Make it four. What did you do? What must be written on the board? Who has an example ready? Recite,—"Two from six leaves four."

Make it eight. What did you do? Who can tell

what to write on the board? Who can give an example? Recite,—"Four and four make eight."

Make it five. How did you do it? What must be written on the board? Who has an example? Recite,—"Three from eight leaves five."

Make it ten. What did you do? What must be written on the board? Who has an example. Recite,—"Five and five make ten."

In giving examples, if the children name the same articles or objects too often, the teacher may ask, who can think of something else? The teacher may also suggest objects, or name them, letting the children supply the numbers and answers.

The board work will be thus :

$$1 + 1 = 2.$$
$$2 + 2 = 4.$$
$$4 - 1 = 3.$$
$$3 + 3 = 6.$$
$$6 - 2 = 4.$$
$$4 + 4 = 8.$$
$$8 - 3 = 5.$$
$$5 + 5 = 10.$$

For seat-work the teacher may erase the signs, and let the children copy upon slates and supply them ; then the answers may be erased and the children required to supply them; then each column of numbers separately.

EXERCISES WITH CARDS TO TEACH ROMAN NUMBERS.

FOR CHILDREN IN FIRST YEAR.

Small boxes containing both Roman and Arabic numbers may be distributed to the children.

The numbers may be painted on the cards, or printed numbers pasted on.

The teacher may make I. on the board, and have the children select one like it from their boxes. If they do not know its name and value, tell them, and have them find the figure 1 and place beside it. Then have them repeat together and separately "I, one."

Then print II. on the board, and have the children find that in their boxes; ask how many letters were made, have them find the figure 2, and repeat "II., two." Proceed with III. in the same way. Ask them to select one, two and three articles, and show the Roman and Arabic numbers. Give the term Roman numbers ; the Arabic may simply be called figures, so as not to confuse the children with hard names. Ask them if they have ever seen Roman numbers used, and where. If they do not know, have them find out if possible ; if not show them.

Then make V. on the board, tell them what it means, have them select it, also the figure 5. Place I. before the V., and tell them it shows one has been taken from the five; ask them how many are left. If they cannot tell, have them find out by objects or marks; then they may select the Roman number and figure four.

Place VI. on the board, point to IV. and ask on which side of the V. the I. is, and what it means; then point to VI. and ask on which side of the V. that I. is; tell them it means that you have added one to the five.

Ask how many it makes, and have them select as before, and so continue with the others.

Review those learned thoroughly before taking up a new number. For the smaller numbers always have the objects counted out, so they will comprehend what the the numbers mean. For review call for different numbers, and have the children hold them up, or place them on their desks; or have them find any number they choose, and when called upon, state what they have.

When the teacher is engaged with another class or grade, the children can busy themselves by arranging the Roman and Arabic numbers in order, as, one, two, three, etc.; by placing the corresponding ones together; and by copying them on their slates.

EXERCISES WITH STICKS TO TEACH ROMAN NUMBERS.

FOR CHILDREN IN FIRST YEAR.

The children may be furnished with two sizes of sticks, one the size of matches, and the other about one-fourth of that size.

The teacher may dictate the numbers to be made, all working together, or certain numbers may be placed on the board for them to represent with their sticks. When they understand the Roman numbers, the Arabic may be written on the board instead of the Roman.

After making the Roman numbers with the sticks, they may copy them on the slates, and write the Arabic numbers by their side, thus furnishing seat-work while the teacher gives attention to another class.

EXERCISES WITH PINS TO TEACH NUMBER.

FOR FIRST YEAR

A copy may be placed on the board, using dots to represent the pin heads. They may be arranged in various positions. Have the children count the dots, and be careful to place the exact number in each position on their cushions.

The pins may also be used in doing little examples in the four rules.

EXERCISES WITH SHOE PEGS TO TEACH NUMBER.

FOR FIRST YEAR AND EXTENDING INTO SECOND YEAR.

Shoe pegs are the most convenient objects to be used in number lessons. They may be bought by the quart at the shoemaker's for a few cents, and may be kept in little bags hung by the seats, to be used as often as necessary.

Boards one-half inch in thickness and six and one-half inches square may be ruled with vertical and horizontal lines one-half an inch apart. Holes may be bored where the lines intersect, large enough to hold shoe pegs.

The children may fill one row with pegs and count them; then two rows, and so on, as they are able to count. They may arrange them in columns of twos, all over the board, leaving a vacant row between, and learn to count them rapidly; then in threes, fours, etc. They may begin with one peg and arrange all the rest in twos, which will give the odd numbers; then leaving the one at the top, arrange in threes; then two at the top, leaving the threes as before. They may be thus taught to make their own addition tables and copy with the appropriate signs plus (+) and equals (=) on their slates. The teacher may write it on the board as the children place their pegs, *they* stating each time what she is to write. After each addition table the subtraction table may be made by taking the same number away each time. Ten times the number added is sufficiently far to go in any of the tables. When the children understand the method, they may make the tables without the teacher's aid, she merely stating what tables they are to make. By glancing over the boards and slates the teacher can readily see whether they are correct.

Little practical examples may be given, and the work done on the board with the pegs. For example : "A boy saved three pennies one day, two pennies the next, and five pennies the next; how many did he save altogether?" They may place three pegs on one row, two pegs on the next, and five pegs on the next; then state "Three pegs (or they may call them pennies) and two pennies are five pennies, and five pennies are ten pennies." Then it may be continued into a subtraction example; as, "He spent one penny, (one peg may be taken up and placed on the other side of the board), then he spent two more pennies, (two pegs may be placed on the other side below the other one) how many pennies had he left? How many did he spend?" They can readily find both answers, as they are right before them. Another kind of an example may be given: "A man planted five trees in a row, and three rows; how many trees were planted?" Let them imagine the pegs are trees, and place them as directed, then count and tell how many trees. Or, "There were four soldiers in a row, and there were five rows; how many soldiers were there ? Five soldiers were shot ; how many were left ?"

In number lessons, children need the objects constantly before them for at least one or two years; and after that they should occasionally be used, especially in teaching new principles. The understanding of all their future work depends upon their correct conception of the value of numbers. If they do not see the results with objects they cannot form any right idea of what they are doing. Therefore the constant use of objects is indispensable, and the greater the variety the better, as it holds their interest, and consequently their attention.

Fractions may be taught to a limited extent by by the use of pegs and blocks. Have the children place two pegs on one side of the board and two on the same row at the other side, and ask how many there are together. Lead them to see that two is one-half of four ; illustrate in various ways and with various things. Then they may place three on each side below the other, and find that three is one-half of six, etc., as far as ten. They may recite "Two and two are four, one-half of four is two; three and three are six, one-half of six is three," etc. They may learn fourths in the same way, and find how many fourths in a half; then thirds, and ninths, and find how many ninths in a third.

Multiplication tables may be made on the boards with pegs. They may place two pegs, below place

EXERCISES WITH SHOE PEGS. 23

two more. Ask how many times they placed two pegs. How many twos have they? How many are two twos? Then place two more and question in same way, and have them recite, "One two is two, two twos are four," etc.

The teacher may tell the children to take a certain number of pegs and find in how many different ways they can arrange them. As the combinations are given they may be written upon the board.

For instance:

$$12 = 6 + 6$$
$$12 = 7 + 5$$
$$12 = 8 + 4$$
$$12 = 9 + 3$$
$$12 = 10 + 2$$
$$12 = 11 + 1$$
$$12 = 4 + 4 + 4$$
$$12 = 3 + 3 + 3 + 3$$
$$12 = 2 + 2 + 2 + 2 + 2 + 2$$
$$12 = 1 + 1 + 1 + 1 + 1 + 1 + 1 + 1 + 1 + 1 + 1 + 1$$
$$12 = 5 + 5 + 2$$
$$12 = 3 + 3 + 6$$
$$12 = 2 + 2 + 8$$
$$12 = 1 + 1 + 10$$
$$12 = 6 + 5 + 1$$
$$12 = 4 + 5 + 3$$
$$12 = 3 + 5 + 4, \text{ etc.}$$

When the idea is gained they may do it by themselves and copy upon their slates. This will keep them employed for a long time.

The pegs may be used without the boards, by

placing them on the slates or desks, and leaving space between the numbers.

Whenever the children are in doubt as to the results of their number lessons, they should be allowed to consult the pegs.

EXERCISES WITH FLAGS TO TEACH NUMBER.

FOR FIRST, SECOND AND THIRD YEARS, ADAPTING AND EXTENDING THE EXERCISES ACCORDING TO ADVANCEMENT OF CHILDREN.

Cut white or colored muslin into four-inch squares and sew them on to small sticks for flags; then paste large numbers on them; the numbers may be printed or cut from old calendars.

Distribute the flags to the class, and have each child in turn tell what number is on his flag, and state all he can about the number; as, "I have number ten; two fives make ten, five twos make ten, five and five make ten, eight and two make ten, seven and three make ten," etc.

The teacher may call upon two of the scholars to stand, and have them add, subtract, multiply, or divide their numbers; or give an example, using the numbers in any way they may think of.

Several may stand, and the teacher may call upon some one to add their numbers very rapidly.

Endeavor to bring as much variety as possible in the exercise; in this way the children learn the value of numbers, and become familiar with all their combinations.

The flags may also be used as a review in Roman numbers, the children stating what Roman number corresponds to the number on their flag.

EXERCISES WITH STICKS TO TEACH NUMERATION.

FOR SECOND AND THIRD YEAR.

A quantity of short sticks (wooden tooth-picks answer nicely) and small rubber bands may be given to the children. They may be told to count out ten sticks and place a rubber band over them. Ask how many sticks they counted. How many bundles made? How many *tens* in one bundle? How many *ones* in one bundle, or one ten?

Have them do up other bundles of tens. Ask them to hold up two tens. How many *ones* in two tens? How many *tens* in twenty ones?

Proceed in the same way with the other bundles until the idea is thoroughly impressed. Then let them count out eleven sticks and ask how many tens. How many left? Have them show eleven, using the bundles.

Call for different numbers between ten and twenty; have them state each time how many *ones*, and how many *tens* and *ones*. Write different numbers on the board, and see if the children can tell how many tens and ones without using the sticks; when mistakes are made let them refer to the sticks, and ascertain by actual count. Dwell thoroughly on different combinations until they are perfect.

Let them do up bundles until they have ten. Have them count the bundles thus: "One ten or ten ones, two tens or twenty ones, three tens or thirty ones," until they have counted ten tens or one hundred ones. Have them place a band around the ten bundles.

Ask how many *ones* in one hundred ? How many *tens* ? They may recite, "One hundred is ten tens or one hundred ones."

For occupation the children may re-count and re-arrange the sticks while the teacher is otherwise engaged.

The children may divide their slates by lines into three parts. Similar divisions may be made on the blackboard. Tell the children that these spaces may be named; the first one on the right may be called *ones*, the second *tens*, and the third *hundreds*.

Have them name the spaces from right to left, and from left to right, many times; then irregularly, pointing them out on their slates as they name them. To help them in remembering the spaces, the first letter of each may be placed at the top of the column.

The teacher may write a number on the board, as 135, in the appropriate spaces. Point to each figure and ask how many ones, tens, and hundreds. Have the children place the corresponding number of *sticks* and *bundles* instead of figures, on their slates in the columns.

Point to the 5, and ask them to hold up the same number of sticks, and then place them on their slates in the right column. Point to the 3, ask them what it is, and what they must hold up. If some make a mistake and hold up the *sticks* instead of *bundles*, question them until they see their mistake. Point to the 1, and ask what kind of bundles must be placed there.

Write 67 on the board under the other figures. Have them place this number, using the sticks upon their slates as before. A line may now be drawn under the numbers on the board ready for addition.

Have them add the sticks in ones' column. Ask them how many sticks or ones. Ask how many tens they can make, and have them do them up in bundles. How many ones left? Where must the ones be placed? What may be written on the board in ones' place? What can be done with the one ten? Write one in tens' column on the board, and have the children place the one bundle with the tens on their slates. Have them add the tens' column in the same way, and find how many hundreds. Place a band around the hundred and place in hundreds' column. As there are no tens left, ask the children what can be placed on the board which means nothing. Have them read the result from their slates and from the board.

It will not be necessary to use the sticks and

bundles on the slates many times. They may soon use the figures referring to the sticks only when puzzled as to the results of the addition.

EXERCISES WITH TOY MONEY TO TEACH SUBTRACTION.

FOR SECOND AND THIRD YEARS.

Boxes of toy money should be distributed among the scholars; where this is impracticable the teacher should have one box for reference on her desk, allowing the scholars to take turns in using it.

Write an example in subtraction on the board, for instance, 342—127. Tell the children they may call the figures money. They may imagine a pocket-book with three divisions. In one division they place pennies, in another dimes, in another dollars. Point to the minuend and tell them that is the amount of money they have in their pocket-book.

They may rule their slates into three parts for the divisions of their purse. Point to the units and ask how many pennies they must place in the first division; then to tens and hundreds. Have them place on their slates two pennies in the first column, four dimes in the second, and three dollars in the third; the remaining money may be left in the box for the "store" or "bank," where change is to be made.

Point to the subtrahend and tell them that is the

amount of money to be paid away. Begin with the pennies and ask how many they have to pay away. How many they have? What can be done when they have not enough pennies? Have they any more money? Have them take one dime from the dime column. Ask what must be done with it. Let them go to the "bank" and change it for pennies. Have them place them with the other pennies and and see how many they have. Now they may pay away the seven pennies and see how many they have left. Do similar work on the board. Ask what they took from the tens. How many left? Cross out the 4 tens and place 3 over it. Ask how many pennies they took for the dime. How many pennies they had altogether. Then place 12 over the 2, and the answer below the line.

Subtract the remaining numbers. When they understand the dimes, use the hundreds in the same way.

Have them make the actual change until they thoroughly understand how and why they do it.

EXERCISES WITH TOY MONEY TO TEACH DIVISION.

FOR THIRD OR FOURTH YEAR.

Distribute the toy money among the children. A simple example in division may be written on the board; (as, 765 ÷ 3). The teacher may point to the dividend and tell the children they may call it money; they may say they have seven dollars, six dimes, and five pennies to divide among three boys.

The scholars may rule their slates in three columns, and place the amount of money in each column as they did in subtraction. Tell them to begin with the dollars and see how many they can give to each boy. Let them take the dollars and place in three piles, having an equal number in each. Ask how many dollars they can give to each boy. How many left? What can be done with the dollar left, can it be divided as it is? If they do not at once see that it must be changed, question them until they do. What must you get for the dollar? How many dimes? Where must you place them?

Have them count the dimes. Let them make three equal piles of the dimes, and see how many each would recive, then place them on the dollar piles. What have you left? What can you do with it? How many pennies will you get? Where will you place them? How many pennies have you now? Make three even piles of the pennies. How many will each receive?

Let them place the pennies on the other piles, count each pile, and find how much money each boy will receive.

When they understand the operation let them do it on their slates, using the figures only, but stating what they do in each step, and why they do it. If they become puzzled let them refer to the money.

Question the children in as many ways as possible about the money. Ask how many pieces of money they had in the beginning. If they cannot answer, ask how many dollars they had. Write the number down. Ask how many dimes. Write that number under the other. Ask how many cents. Place that number under the others and add. In the same way have them count the number of pieces given to each boy. To how many did they give this number ? How may the total number be found ? They will find they have given away more pieces than they had in the beginning. Ask how that is. If they cannot tell, take a dime and ask how it could be given away in two pieces. In ten pieces.

EXERCISES WITH TOY MONEY TO TEACH THE VALUE OF REAL MONEY.

FOR THIRD YEAR.

Provide each child with a box of toy-money, which can be obtained from book or toy stores. Have the children learn the names of the different coins, if they do not already know them. Show the real money, and talk about the material of which it is made. Their previous lessons will enable them to tell something about it, and where obtained. Speak of the process of its manufacture into money. Tell them the name of the place where the coins are stamped. Call their attention to the impressions on each.

Ask them to lay out two pennies, then *one* piece of the same value; also five pennies, and *one* piece of the same value; and in this way find the value of all the coins to one dollar. Beans or stones may be substituted for pennies for the higher denominations. Then use two-cent pieces in connection with the pennies, then threes, fives, etc., making all conceivable combinations, until the children are thoroughly acquainted with their value, and can readily substitute the correct number of small coins for the larger ones.

Give the children easy practical examples to solve, using the money; for example: "If John goes to the store and buys two cents' worth of candy, and gives a five-cent piece, how much change ought he to receive?" If they cannot tell readily, let them lay out five pennies and take two away. When they are able to solve the simplest examples readily, take more difficult ones, combining addition and subtraction, also multiplication and division. Whenever the children are puzzled, let them use the beans or blocks, and work it all out for themselves. It would be well to provide each child with a small bag of beans. The children should all work in concert, as they are all furnished with the materials. Call upon different ones to explain the examples. If any of the children are able, let them give questions to the class.

Teach them to make change rapidly and in a business way.

"If I give a fifty-cent piece for three yards of ribbon, at nine cents a yard, how much change should I receive?"

Have them say, "Twenty-seven and three are thirty, and ten are forty, and ten are fifty;" have them pick up the money as they mention each piece.

This will require a great deal of drill to make them expert.

Cards may be prepared by the teacher, having figures and signs written upon them. These may be distributed to the scholars, and they may be taught to make up mental examples from them.

This exercise will compel the children to think, affording at the same time a temporary rest for the teacher.

The following will explain the plan proposed:

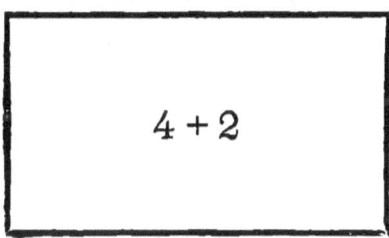

The above represents the card which the child receives. He may say, "If I have four pencils, and my brother gives me two more, I shall then have six pencils."

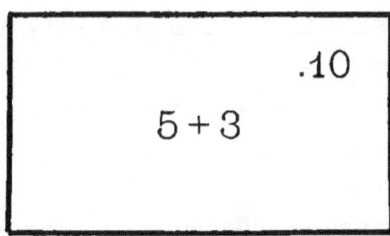

"If I spend five cents for candy, and three cents for nuts, I shall spend eight cents; if I give a ten-cent piece for them, I ought to receive two cents in change."

$$7-3$$

"If John had seven marbles, and lost three of them, he would have four marbles left."

$$7+4-5$$

"If James earned seven cents one day, and four cents another day, he would earn in all eleven cents; if he spent five cents for ribbon, he would have six cents left."

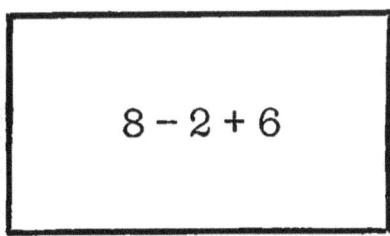

"If Clara had eight paper dolls and lost two of them, she would have six dolls remaining; if she bought six more dolls she would then have twelve dolls."

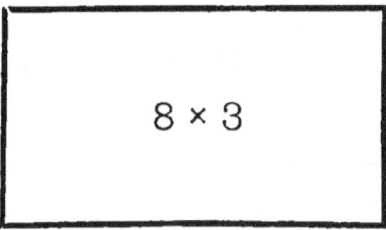

"If one banana cost eight cents, three bananas would cost twenty-four cents."

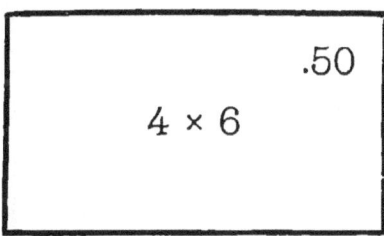

"If I pay six cents for one slate, for four slates I must pay twenty-four cents; if I give a fifty-cent piece for them, I shall receive twenty-six cents change."

$$14 \div 7$$

"If seven tops cost fourteen cents, one top will cost two cents."

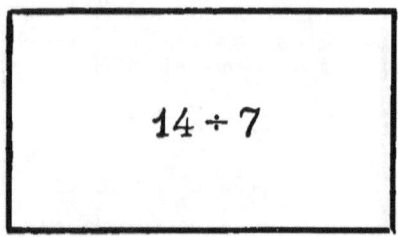

"If four kites cost sixteen cents, one kite will cost four cents; if I buy one and give a twenty-five-cent piece, I shall receive twenty-one cents change."

$$72 \div 9 \times 3$$

"If nine pounds of starch cost seventy-two cents, one pound will cost eight cents; if one pound cost eight cents, three pounds will cost twenty-four cents."

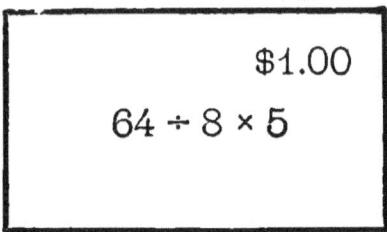

"If eight pictures cost sixty-four cents," etc.

$$17 + 7 \div 4$$

"If I had seventeen cents, and my father gave me seven more cents, I should have twenty-four cents; I could get as many lemons at four cents a piece as four cents is contained times into twenty-four cents, which is six times."

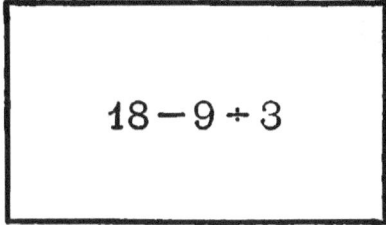

"If I had eighteen cents, and spent nine," etc.

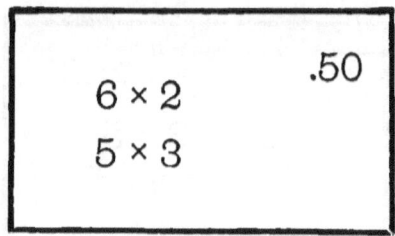

"If I pay six cents for one paper of needles, for two papers I must pay twelve cents; if 1 pay five cents for one paper of pins, for three papers I must pay fifteen cents; and the two together will cost twenty-seven cents. If I give a fifty-cent piece for them, I shall receive," etc.

$$1772 - 1706$$

"If a man were born in 1706 and died in 1772, his age would be the difference between 1772 and 1706, which is sixty-six years."

$$1768 - 59$$

"If a man died in 1768 at the age of 59, the year

in which he was born would be the difference between 1768 and 59, which is 1709."

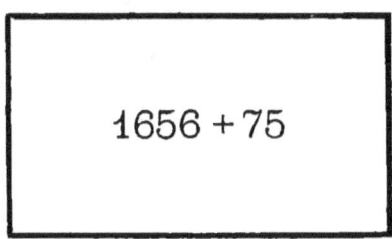

"If a man were born in 1656 and lived 75 years, the year that he died would be the sum of 1656 and 75, which is 1731."

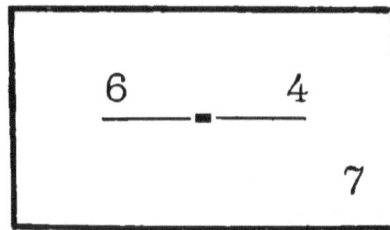

"If two men start from the same place and travel in opposite directions, one at the rate of six miles a day and the other at the rate of four miles a day, at the end of one day they would be ten miles apart, and at the end of seven days they would be seventy miles apart."

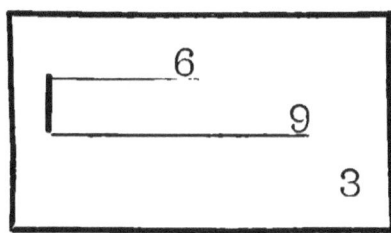

"If two men start from the same place, and go in the same direction—one at the rate of six miles a day, and the other at the rate of nine miles a day—at the end of one day they would be three miles apart," etc.

EXERCISES WITH CLOCK-DIALS TO TEACH TIME.

FOR SECOND YEAR.

The children may each be provided with a clock-dial, which may be made in the following manner: Take paste-board or boxes and cut into pieces about eight inches square. With a string and very dark pencil make two large circles about one inch apart on each; between these circles make the Roman numbers as found on the clock; making the minute marks between. Cut out paste-board hands, fasten two, the minute and hour, in the centre of each, just loose enough to be moved with ease.

The teacher may have a clock for her own use, or make the dial on the board or on card-board similar to the children's.

The teacher may ask what the cards represent and what kind of numbers found on them.

The children may point to the Roman numbers, naming each.

The teacher may then ask the children to name some length of time, and then ask how that is repre-

EXERCISES WITH CLOCK-DIALS. 41

sented on the clock; or ask the shortest period of time and refer to the second hand of her watch; then the next longer period and how that is represented. Ask what number they must count to take a minute of time. Ask how long a second is; what they could do in a second. Refer to pendulum; show by vibrating something, so they will comprehend the length of time. Ask how many seconds make a minute. What part of the clock points to the time; what difference they notice in the hands; which hand points to the minute. Ask for the next longer period of time; how many minutes the long hand has to point to before it is an hour; how far around the clock it goes; how far for a half hour, for a quarter, for three-quarters; let them count the minutes in each. If an even hour, ask where the minute hand would be; if a half-hour, quarter, etc. Which is the hour hand? Have them point to each and tell their names.

Ask where the hour hand would be at each successive hour. If twelve o'clock where each hand would be; if one, two, three, etc. Have them tell how far the hour hand goes on the clock in one hour; how far the minute hand travels in same time. Ask how many hours in one day; how many times the hour hand goes round in the day; the minute hand? Which hand goes fast? Which slow? What does the fast hand show? the slow hand?

Then have them set the hands at twelve; what time? at one, etc. Ask different ones what time it is and where the hands are. In setting even hours, which is the only hand to move? Then drill on half hours, quarters, five minutes, etc.

For review have all set certain time, and ask where hands are. Then let them set their own time, and state time and position of hands.

This may be taught to quite young children. The time table may be written on the board and learned by the children.

Show them how railroad time is given and written, and drill on it both orally and written.

Ask of what materials watches and clocks are made; how they are made to go; what has to be done to make them go. Give them some idea of the spring and wheels.

State the difference between clocks and watches.

Show a sun dial if possible, and tell them how time is told by that; how the correct time is known.

EXERCISES WITH RULES TO TEACH LONG MEASURE.

FOR THIRD YEAR.

Furnish each child with a foot rule, and a slip of paper one inch in length. The teacher may have a yard-stick. Tell the children the length of the rules and the papers. Let them lay their slips of paper on their rules and find for themselves how many inches in a foot. Lay the yard-stick down, and let

EXERCISES WITH RULES. 43

them place their rules on it to ascertain how many feet make a yard.

Let them find the inch-marks on the rules and on the yard-stick, and count the number of inches in a yard.

Have them fold their inch slips in half, and find the half-inch on their rules. Ask how many half-inches in an inch.

Let them fold their slips again and tell the number of parts, also find the length on their rules.

Halve and quarter a number of different objects in the presence of the children, so they may thoroughly comprehend that two halves, or four quarters, make a whole thing.

Let one child find one-half of the yard, and see how many inches. Let another find one-quarter of the yard, and see how many inches. If they have difficulty in finding the half or quarter of the yard, let them take a string or slip of paper one yard in length, and fold it—once for the half, and twice for the quarter.

Let them also find the number of inches in one-half and one-quarter of a foot.

In what stores are these measures used? Give the term Long Measure. What goods are sold by it? What other persons use it? Refer to carpenters, masons, builders, tailors, and dress-makers.

The portion of the table that they have found may now be written upon the board and learned by the children.

BLACKBOARD LESSON.

12 inches	make	1	foot.
6 "	"	$\frac{1}{2}$	"
3 "	"	$\frac{1}{4}$	"
3 feet	"	1	yard.
36 inches	"	1	"
18 "	"	$\frac{1}{2}$	"
9 "	"	$\frac{1}{4}$	"

Long Measure is used in dry-goods and fancy-stores; it is also used by carpenters, builders, masons, tailors, and dress-makers.

It is used to measure cloth, muslin, flannel, calico, silk, velvet, ribbon, braid, lace, wood, etc.

Teach the children to test length by the eye, beginning with the inch.

For occupation without the teacher's aid, the children may be supplied with slips of paper (narrow slips that come from ribbons do nicely, and may be procured from fancy-stores), which they may measure off in half-inches, inches, quarter and half feet, and quarter and half yards, marking the length of each with a lead-pencil; by folding and creasing the paper it may be easily and nicely torn.

This exercise will help to fix the lengths in their minds, and assist them greatly in testing them.

Have them measure many things in the schoolroom and out of it, and set the dimensions down on a slate or piece of paper, thus : "The slate is six inches long and four inches wide;" or, "The slate is 6 x 4 inches."

Teach them to be trusted, and let one or more go with rules to different parts of the room, building or yard, and measure certain things and set it down, with the names of the objects attached. Let others measure the same things and compare. In measuring long distances, let them take a piece of chalk and mark off.

This exercise may be granted as a favor for faithfulness.

EXERCISES WITH WEIGHTS TO TEACH AVOIRDUPOIS WEIGHT.

FOR THIRD YEAR.

The teacher may have scales and all the different sizes of weights to a pound.

Let the children name some weights. Have some one find the pound-weight and place it on the scales; let some one find two weights that will exactly balance it; then four, and eight. Have them tell what names to give to the weights when two are equal to a pound, when four, and when eight. Their previous lessons will help them to answer these questions.

Have them find the smallest weight, and tell them its name if they do not know. Have them find how many ounces make a quarter of a pound, and have them tell from that how many make a half, three-quarters, and a pound.

Give them the name Avoirdupois Weight. Ask

in what stores it is used. Name the articles weighed by it.

BLACKBOARD LESSON.

16 ounces make 1 pound.
8   "   " $\frac{1}{2}$ "
4   "   " $\frac{1}{4}$ "
12 "   " $\frac{3}{4}$ "

Avoirdupois Weight is used in grocery, butcher, bakery, and candy stores.

It is used to weigh tea, coffee, sugar, crackers, cheese, butter, meat, raisins, prunes, figs, cherries, spices, etc.

The children should be allowed to weigh different quantities of beans, sand, or any other convenient article. They should be taught to be particular about the exact balance. They may put the articles weighed in paper-bags, mark them any article they choose, set the price and figure the amount.

EXERCISES WITH MEASURES TO TEACH LIQUID MEASURE.

FOR THIRD YEAR.

The teacher should be furnished with a gill, pint, quart, and gallon measures, also a box of beans or sand.

The children may be asked to name some measure they know, and point it out; with that for a starting-point, proceed to the other measures. If a quart is first selected, let another child find another measure, and tell, if he knows, what it is. Then let him find out for himself, by measuring the sand or beans, how many of one make the other. If a gallon is next selected, let some one see how many times he can fill the quart and pour into the gallon, the children watching and counting.

Proceed in the same way with the other measures. They will thus learn by actual experiment how many gills make a pint, quart, and gallon; and how many pints make a quart and gallon.

The teacher may supply the name of the measure when the children do not know. The pint, quart, and gallon measure may be marked to indicate the half and quarter. Then the children may find by measuring how many of each lower denomination it takes to make the half and quarter of the higher.

Ask what articles are measured with these measures. Who use them? What is this measure called?

BLACKBOARD LESSON.—LIQUID MEASURE.

4 gills make 1 pint.
2 pints " 1 quart.
4 quarts " 1 gallon.
1 gill " $\frac{1}{4}$ pint.
2 " " $\frac{1}{2}$ "
3 " " $\frac{3}{4}$ "
1 pint " $\frac{1}{2}$ quart.
1 quart " $\frac{1}{4}$ gallon.
2 " " $\frac{1}{2}$ "
3 " " $\frac{3}{4}$ "

Liquid Measure is used by grocers, milkmen, liquor-dealers, and house-keepers. It is used to measure milk, vinegar, cider, oil, molasses, syrup, liquors, etc.

EXERCISES WITH BLOCKS TO TEACH POSITION.

FOR FIRST YEAR.

Furnish each child with a stout bag containing eight cubes and one square prism three times the length of a cube.

Cubes one and a half or two inches square are a very good size. These blocks may be obtained, with slight expense, from the carpenter. The bags can be made by the older children.

Have the children stand up their long blocks and point to the front, back, right, and left hand sides, top and bottom of them.

When this is well understood, have them place two blocks in front, two back, and two on right and left hand sides of the long blocks; then have them take out the long blocks, and ask what they have made. If no idea is suggested to them, tell them to call it a well, which they will be pleased to imagine. A conversation may follow concerning wells. How many have seen wells? Where? Do we see them in cities? What is found in them? How is the water obtained? From where does the water come? What are the uses of water?

What would happen if we had no water? It would be well for the teacher to have several drawings on the board, illustrating the different ways in which water is drawn.

When this subject is exhausted, have them cover the wells with the long blocks, and take away the two front blocks, when a fire-place will be formed. Tell them about the old-fashioned fire-places. Show a picture of one. Make a drawing of and-irons supporting burning logs. Let them find the mantel over the fire-place, and talk about that.

Then have them remove the two back blocks, and a bridge will be found. Another conversation may now follow concerning the materials used in building bridges, their uses, what is found under them, what is found in the water, how fish are caught, kinds of fish, etc. Is water always found under bridges? Refer to roads and railroads.

Two blocks may be placed under the bridge, and a wall is suggested. Let the children tell of what materials walls are made; when of stone, how the heavy stones are carried; when of bricks, what is placed between them to keep them firmly together; of what that is made, and of what bricks are made. Ask of what use walls are.

The long blocks may be taken off and placed in front at the base of the wall, when a settee will appear. Question concerning the material, use, and where used.

The long blocks may be removed, the middle ones

separated and placed before the remaining ones, when two chairs will be found. Let the children name them, as father's and mother's, or brother's and sister's.

Place one block on the back of each, and grandfather's and grand-mother's chairs are made.

The blocks may be arranged to form steps, and the ordinals may be taught. The teacher may point to one step, and ask which step is touched; then point to another, and so continue until all have been touched. Then have the children point and recite, "first, second, third," etc., until all have been named forward and backward.

When the teacher is not with the class, they may be allowed to build anything their fancies dictate.

EXERCISES WITH SHOE PEGS TO TEACH FORM.

FOR FIRST YEAR.

Shoe pegs may be distributed among the children. They may arrange them in straight lines in every position—curved, crooked, broken, waved, spiral, circles, arcs, angles, triangles, and all the plain figures.

They may form letters, numbers, and Roman numbers.

Designs, as in drawing, may be made, windows, picture-frames, chairs, trees, flowers, birds, houses, and animals.

The teacher may at first draw the outlines of the objects on the board, using short marks to represent the pegs. When the idea is gained they may work by themselves, and when called upon be able to tell something about the object, its material, use, etc.; or, it may be, relate a little story in connection with it.

Children are interested in what they form for themselves. Their imaginations are lively, and they will readily picture in their mind the objects, no matter how rough or crude the representation.

Dyeing the pegs will add greatly to the children's pleasure.

EXERCISES WITH PINS TO TEACH FORM.
FOR FIRST AND SECOND YEARS.

The children may be furnished with small, plain pin-cushions, made of strong, dark material, a narrow strip of the same material, several inches long, filled with pins, may be securely fastened to one corner of each cushion.

The teacher may speak of the materials of pins, and have the children find their parts. Ask what part of the pin they put in the cushion first, with what part they push it, and what part is between the head and point. Ask about the shape of the head, and what can be said of the point. Compare the point with a blunt pencil or stick; if the term *sharp* is not given, prick the hands lightly. Bend a pin and then compare it with a good one to get the term straight.

They may recite, "The pin has a head, shank, and point; the head is round, the shank is straight, and the point is sharp."

Speak of some of the processes of manufacture, and of the number of different persons employed in making so small an article.

Let them state the various uses of pins. The pins may be arranged on the cushions in the forms of letters, numbers, Roman numbers, all the positions of lines and angles, and all the different forms.

Copies of things may be made on the board, dots being used to represent the heads of the pins. If the children find difficulty in placing the pins in right positions, the teacher may mark the pattern with chalk upon the cushions and let them follow the lines. It would be well to teach them to make their own initials, as soon as they are capable.

When the children are able to arrange the forms, they may be told to make certain figures, as a circle with a pin or cross in the center; a square with a circle in it, etc. Various designs will suggest themselves.

This exercise will make pleasant and useful occupation for the smaller children, while the teacher is busy with the older ones.

EXERCISES WITH STICKS TO TEACH POSITION OF LINES.

FOR SECOND YEAR.

Provide each child with several short sticks (about the size of matches*); these may be kept either in small boxes, giving one to each child, or in one large box, from which they may be distributed.

The teacher may take a stick and hold it in a vertical position, ask the children each to take a stick and do the same. Ask some one to draw a line to look like the stick as he is holding it. Let them find several things in the room in the same position. Tell them this position is called vertical.

Ask some one to stand in a vertical position, or hold slate or book in same position. Have the class repeat, "I hold my stick in a vertical position. I hold my slate," etc."

When this is learned, the teacher may hold the stick in a horizontal position, asking the children to do the same. Place the slates horizontal. Have them draw this line on the board, and find objects in the room in same position. Give the term horizontal.

In what position are the walls? The ceiling? The floor? The legs of the table? The top of the table?

---

* Wooden tooth-picks may be bought by the box (500 or more) for about ten cents.

The slanting position may next be taken, and term given.

What part of the desk is slanting? What part of the house? In what position are the easel and blackboard?

Place two or more sticks parallel, and have them do the same. Lead them to see that the lines will never meet. Let them find as many parallel lines as possible in the room. Then let them place the sticks forming vertical, horizontal, and slanting parallel lines, and find objects in each position.

After the oral lesson, the children may arrange the sticks by themselves, and copy the positions on their slates.

EXERCISES WITH STICKS TO TEACH ANGLES.
FOR SECOND YEAR.

Review quickly the preceding lessons on lines; have the children work in concert and see that all thoroughly understand the directions. If any of the children are dull or inattentive call upon them the most frequently.

The teacher may now take a pocket-knife and open the blade half-way, then ask the children to place two of their sticks in the same position. Hold the knife thus opened in every conceivable position, asking the children to change their sticks in like positions. Have the children find the opening between the sticks, and give the term, angle.

EXERCISES WITH STICKS. 55

Ask how far open the knife is, and how they have made their angles to look. Tell them that, "An angle that looks like a knife half-way open is called a *right angle*."

Lead them to see that it is still a right angle in whatever position it may be held or made.

Ask some one to come to the board and make a right angle, then some one else to make one in a different position, and continue until all the positions have been made. If they fail to find a new position, show them with the knife and let them copy; when not quite sure whether it is an exact right angle, let them take the knife and measure it.

Be careful to teach *accuracy* in observation and work.

Now let the children find all the right angles in the room. Let them place their slates at right angles with the desk, floor, or wall; also place their arms at right angles with their bodies, thus testing in every possible way to fix it in their memories.

When this is mastered, close the knife a little and ask the children to form the same with their sticks. Call attention to the size. Is it larger or smaller than the right angle? Give the term *acute* or *sharp*.

Let them repeat, "An angle smaller than a right angle is called an *acute angle*."

Lead them to see that acute angles may be of different sizes so long as they are less than a right angle.

Let them make these in all positions and sizes, and find similar ones in the room.

Then open the knife further than half-way, again refer to size, and give the term *obtuse* or *blunt*.

Have them repeat, "An angle larger than a right angle is called an *obtuse angle*." Have them make the obtuse angle in all positions and sizes, and find any there may be in the room.

Now have the children place their sticks, so as to form two right angles, ⊥ ; four right angles, ┼ ; one obtuse and one acute angle, ∠ ; two obtuse and two acute angles, ✕ ; and if possible find the same positions in objects in the room. This will teach them to observe closely.

For a review in angles, have the children use the sticks to form all the large letters of the alphabet composed of straight lines. Have the children find all the angles in each letter, tell what kind, and how many of each.

EXERCISES WITH WIRE TO TEACH CURVED LINES.

FOR SECOND YEAR.

Provide the children with short pieces of stiff, yet pliable wire. Ask them what they can do with their wires that they could not do with their sticks.

EXERCISES WITH PINS. 57

Ask them to bend their wires in different positions. Have them make similar lines on the board. Try to have them make all the positions themselves—as curved, crooked, broken, waved, spiral, circle, and half or semi-circle. If they do not get them readily, direct their attention to objects which contain them. Show a ring, arch, spring, draw a spider's web, waves, etc. Refer to straight parallel lines, and then ask for curved parallel lines.

EXERCISES WITH OBJECTS TO TEACH SURFACES.

FOR SECOND YEAR.

The teacher may be provided with a box of forms, and each child with a bag, containing blocks, balls, marbles, tops, and beans.

First, develop the idea of outside. Open the box of forms and ask where the blocks are. When the term inside has been given, close the box, and ask what part of the box they now see; or place the hands over the box, touching all parts of it, and ask what part is touched. When the term outside has been given, give the statement: "The outside of anything is called the surface."

Have the children touch the surface of their blocks, marbles, tops, books, slates, and desks.

Ask the children to roll their balls or marbles; then ask them to roll their blocks. Why cannot the blocks be rolled like the balls or marbles? If they fail to give the term, ask some one to draw the ball on the board; another the block.

What lines were used in drawing the block? In drawing the ball? If the ball has a curved line, what shall we say of its surface? What could we do with the balls that we could not do with the blocks? State—"A surface that will roll is called a curved surface."

Have the children find all the curved surfaces among their own objects, then select them from the box of forms.

Ask the children to touch one part of the surface of their blocks, another, and another; see how many parts they can find. State—"A part of the surface is called a face."

How many faces have the blocks?—the books?—the slates?—the balls?—the marbles?

Compare the faces of the cube with the ball, marble and cone. State—"Some faces are curved and some are plain."

What kind of a face has the slate?—the doorknob?—the cup?—the globe?—the egg?—the desk?

Ask them to touch the place where the faces meet. Refer to the edge of the desk, table, and chair. State—"The place where the faces meet is called the edge." Compare the straight and curved edges. State—"Some edges are straight and some are curved."

Have them find the two kinds of edges among the forms and objects in the room. Ask them to find the place where the edges meet on their blocks and other objects. State—"The place where the edges meet is called the corner."

Have them find all the corners they can.

EXERCISE WITH CLAY TO TEACH FORM.

If practicable, provide each child with a small piece of board containing wet clay. Where the class is too large, have a large tray or box containing the clay, and allow two or three children to work at one time, while the class look on, and criticise the work. When necessary, different ones may be appointed to rectify mistakes; thus all may be kept interested.

As in previous lessons, begin with a talk about clay. What kind of a substance? Where obtained? Of what use? Speak of bricks; have one to show. If convenient, present other objects made of clay; speak of their manufacture, or what is better, let the children find out as much as possible for themselves, and relate at the next lesson.

Have the children first make a ball or sphere of clay. What kind of a surface has it? How many hemispheres can be made of it? Let them cut it with a knife. What part of the sphere is the hemisphere? What does *hemi* mean? How many halves in a sphere? in an apple? in anything? How many faces has it? What kind? What edges? Let them place the two halves together, then press it, and make an oblate-spheroid; then make it round again, and taper one end for an ovate-spheroid or egg-shape. Return again to the sphere, and cut off each side for a cube. Review the shape as to faces, edges and corners. Roll it out for a cylinder, cut off sides for square prism; if possible cut it in two for triangular prism. Then form pyramids, cones, etc.

Let them make the shapes of different kinds of fruit, using little sticks for stems; for strawberries they could make little indentures with pins for the seeds. Have a talk about each kind of fruit, and when practicable, present the natural.

Have a lesson on the bird's nest, and let them mould it in clay, and make the eggs and place in it. Let them give a list of the names of little birds. A great variety of objects can be made, as well as cakes, pies and bread, and a little lesson on each be given. The children will exercise their own ingenuity and devise many new forms.

EXERCISES WITH STICKS TO TEACH PLANE FIGURES.

FOR SECOND YEAR.

Ask the children to make a right angle and enclose it with a third stick.

How many sticks did you use?

How many angles have you made?

How many sides has the figure.

EXERCISES WITH STICKS.

State—"A figure having three sides and three angles is called a *triangle; tri* means three."

Always be careful to develop the idea before giving the term, and in giving the definition, to place the term at the end.

In forming this triangle, ask them what angle they made first. Define, "A triangle that has a right angle is called a *right-angled triangle.*"

Have the children turn it around in various positions to see that it still remains a right-angled triangle. Ask what the other angles are.

Have them make an obtuse angle and form into a triangle. Define, "An angle that has an obtuse angle is called an *obtuse-angled triangle.*"

What other angles has this triangle? Have them make an acute angle and convert into a triangle. What kind of angles has this triangle? Define, "A triangle that has three acute angles is called an *acute-angled triangle.*"

Have them select from the box of forms all the triangles, tell what kind they are, and how they know.

If practicable, give them pieces of paper and small blunt scissors, and let them cut out all the different triangles. If this cannot be done in school, let them do it at home and bring to school.

Next proceed to the square. Point to one in the room or draw one on the board, and let them copy with their sticks. How many angles has this? What kind? How many sides? What can you say of the sides? If they do not give the right term, have them measure the sides. Define, "A figure that has four equal sides and four right angles is called a *square*."

Have them divide the square obliquely and tell what they find. Then let them divide it across, and question as to the angles, sides, and length of sides.

Give definition, "A figure that has four right angles and four sides, two of which are longer than the other two, is called an *oblong*."

In what are the square and oblong alike? In what are they different?

Refer to objects in the room, such as slates, books, desks, windows, doors, tables, paper and envelopes.

Then proceed in a similar manner to form the rhomb, rhomboid, trapezoid, trapezium, pentagon, hexagon, heptagon, octagon, etc.

EXERCISES WITH PAPER TO TEACH FORM.
FOR SECOND YEAR.

Furnish the children with short, narrow pieces of colored paper and cards, or small pieces of pasteboard or box-covers, the size of cards. Dissolve five cents' worth of gum tragacanth in a bowl of water, and pour into small butter-plates, placing one plate for the use of every two children.

The children may paste the papers on their cards, using all the positions of straight lines, angles, and figures enclosed with straight lines which they have learned. The teacher may have these previously drawn upon the board for the children to copy.

As it will take many days for them to finish their sets, they may have small rubber bands to slip over their cards; the top cards may have their names written upon them, that they may have their own package another time. When a set is completed it may be laid aside for review, and at the close of the term given to the child.

When the children become expert in this work, they may be furnished with muslin scrap-books, which when filled may be laid aside for exhibition.

EXERCISES WITH SHOE-PEGS IN TEACHING FORM AND NUMBER.

FOR SECOND YEAR.

The children may arrange the pegs on the boards* in all the forms of plain figures, and when called upon, be able to tell the forms and the number of pegs used in each.

The plain figures may be drawn upon the board, the children may make them with the pegs on their boards, then copy them upon their slates, writing by each form the number of pegs used in making it.

They may also make the same designs and forms that they make with the pegs without the boards.

They may imagine the board to be a garden,

* Mentioned in the previous chapter on Number.

which they may fence with the pegs, by placing a row all around the outside; they may make gateways and paths. They may plant flowers by placing two or three pegs in one hole, or by placing small pieces of colored papers on the pegs. When called upon they may tell how many pegs are in their fence, and name the different kinds of flowers they have planted. The teacher may suggest a particular season and have them plant flowers appropriate to it.

For variety, they may have vegetables or trees instead of flowers. They may be left to amuse themselves in this way when the teacher is otherwise employed.

EXERCISES WITH BLOCKS IN TEACHING SOLID FIGURES.

FOR LATTER PART OF SECOND OR FIRST PART OF THIRD YEAR.

Review the previous lessons on surfaces (page 57). Have each one take a cube and count the faces. Compare the faces of the cube with the marble or ball, and ask what kind of faces it has. What shape are its faces? How many edges has it? What kind of edges? How many corners? State—"The cube has six plain, square faces, twelve straight edges, and eight corners."

Present a square prism and have them count the faces, edges, and corners. What is the difference between the prism and cube? If they do not readily tell the difference, call attention to the oblong faces. Have them count the oblong faces and the square faces. State—"A square prism has four plain oblong faces, two plain square faces, twelve straight edges, and eight corners."

Present the triangular prism, and have them count all the faces. Have them notice the shapes of the faces, and tell the number of each. Place the square and triangular prisms together and call the attention of the scholars to the ends of each. Point to the square prism and ask what shape the end is; then ask its name. Point to the triangular prism and ask its shape, and what name could be given to it. State—"A triangular prism has three plain oblong faces, two plain triangular faces, nine straight edges, and six corners."

The hexagonal prism may be treated in a similar manner. When it has been thoroughly examined, state—"A hexagonal prism has six plain oblong faces, two plain hexagonal faces, eighteen straight edges, and twelve corners."

The cylinder may now be examined. Let the children see how many and what kinds of faces and edges it has, and state, "The cylinder has one curved face, two plain faces, and two curved edges."

The pyramids may be shown. Let some one find the point where the faces touch, and give the term apex; some one else touch the part on which it stands, and give the term base. Speak of the Pyramids of Egypt. Have them count and describe the faces and edges of the square and triangular pyramids. State—"The square pyramid has one square plain face called the base, four triangular plain faces meeting in a point called the apex, and eight straight edges." "The triangular prism has one triangular plain face called the base, three triangular plain faces which meet in a point called the apex, and six straight edges."

NOTE. These forms may be made of pasteboard and covered with colored paper.

EXERCISES WITH MOULDING-BOARD TO TEACH GEOGRAPHY.

FOR SECOND AND THIRD YEARS.

Have a board 4x5 feet made, with a rim around the edge an inch high. Upon this board, which should be adjusted to a table or desk, put half a bushel of moulding sand, such as may be had from a foundry; or, if this is impracticable, a half-bushel of moist loam, sifted, will answer the purpose well. With the use of blocks, toy-houses, trees, animals, large and small pieces of looking-glass, green tissue paper, narrow blue ribbon or tape, small twigs for evergreen trees, shells, and stones, the principal definitions in geography may be practically and impressibly taught.

When the class is small, it is best to have all the scholars gather around the moulding-board; but where the class is large, a part may gather around the board, while the others observe and suggest. The teacher should be careful to give every pupil his proportion of time at the moulding-board.

SEA-SHORE.—Place a large piece of looking-glass on one side of the moulding-board, and fill the rest with sand.

Tell the children you will have a talk with them about the earth or world in which they live.

On what do the ships sail? On what are houses built? What two things are found on the earth? What have we to represent the water on this board? What the land? Who will find the place where the water and land come together? Does any one know what we call the place where the land touches the water? Give the term coast or shore. When sailors go far-off on the water, where do we say they have gone? What may we call this water? What may we call this shore or coast? How many have ever been to the sea-shore? How does the water of the sea taste? If they do not know, place some salt in water and have them taste it. Of what use is the sea? Speak of the water rising, forming into clouds, and returning in rain. Could we live without water? What is the water always doing? Show a picture where waves are represented. If you were close by the sea-shore, on what would you be standing? Show pictures of both sandy and rocky seashores. What name do we give to a sandy sea-shore? What are found on the beach? Let some one place shells on the beach. Some one else make part of it rocky by placing rough stones on it. What is found on the rocks? Show sea-weed, if possible. What are found on some rocks deep in the water? Present sponges. Tell them how they are obtained. Would you like to sail around this coast on a dark, stormy night? Show a picture of a shipwreck. What might happen to the ship? What do people build on the coast to help the sailors? Show a picture of a lighthouse. Let some one build a lighthouse with blocks. What do people put out on the water that floats, to direct sailors? Speak of buoys. Speak of the life-saving service. Name some things found in the water. How do people get shell-fish? What time of year do people like to visit the seashore? Why? What do many people go for in the warm weather? What kind of a coast is best for bathing?

This conversation includes several lessons. It is given in full to show how the lessons may be given. It may be improved upon according to the ability of the teacher.

MOUNTAINS AND VALLEYS.—Let one of the children pile up the sand at one end of the moulding-board. Who can give a name for what has been made? Who will make it a very high hill? Can any one give this a name? Show me from what part of it you could see the farthest. Give the term *summit*. If you were going up the mountain, show where you would begin to climb. Give the term *base.* In going from the base to the summit, show me over what part you would journey. Give the term *sides.* What would you be likely to find on the sides of the mountain? Show picture of a mountain with trees. Let the children plant the sprigs of evergreen in a portion of the sides. What do we call a place where there are a great many trees? Very large woods have another name. Give term *forest.* Name some forest trees. If you were going to climb a mountain, what would you take in your hand to help you? Why? If you were thirsty, what would you hunt for? Where does the water of a spring come from? How does it taste? What would you find running from the spring? What name would we give it? What would you find in the bottom of the brook? How could you cross the brook? What does the brook do that children do? What part of the mountain is the coldest? Do you know what is found on the tops of very high mountains? Let some one place cotton on the top for snow. Are the sides of the mountains always covered with trees? Show picture of a rocky mountain. Place stones on the sides where the trees were not placed. How many ever found large holes among the rocks? Let them form a cave with the stones. Speak of wild animals and their houses. Speak of some of the wonderful caves. Relate stories—historical or other. If we were going to climb the mountain, show me the direction we would take. How many think we would go straight up?

Why not? Show a winding-path in the mountain. Show picture where mules are used. What animal is in the picture? Why is the mule or donkey used instead of a horse. Make a narrow, winding path up the mountain. What do people find by digging down into the mountain? If possible have ore to show. Coal at least can be presented. Show picture of a mine, and have a talk about it. Loosen part of the sand, and show what sometimes happens on the mountains; have a few houses in the way of the avalanche. If people wanted to go by cars from one side of the mountain to another, where would the railroad be built? Why around instead of over? If they wanted to go the nearest way, or if there were many mountains and no low valleys, how could they manage? Show picture of a tunnel. If possible, make one. Let some one form another mountain. Have some one find the place between. Ask what it is called. Where would the greater number of houses be, on the mountain or in the valley? Why? What birds like to build their nests among the rocks of mountains? Show the eagle and nest. What animals like to climb the mountains? Show pictures of the deer, chamois, goats and sheep. Relate stories of the travelers in the Alps.

VOLCANO.—Have children make a mountain. The teacher may make a hole in it, and place a burning candle. What shall we call this kind of a mountain? How many would like to live on such a mountain? Why not? Speak of Vesuvius and the buried cities. Show pumice-stone.

DESERT.—Have the sand leveled off, with nothing upon it. Tell the children there are places on the earth where, as far as they could see, there would be nothing but sand. Does any one know the name of such a place? If no one does, give the term *desert*. Would people build houses in such a place? Why not? What is one of the things that we cannot live without? Tell them of the necessity of traveling sometimes in such countries, of the kind of animals used, and why. Show a picture of a camel. Speak of his feet, his bag for carrying water, and his hump for storing away his fat. Speak of the kind of food people carry in the desert, and the leather bottles they use for water. Speak of the oases, and make them by planting a few trees and placing a small glass for the spring. Show picture of palm trees, and speak of their multiplicity of uses. Mention the wind storms, and pile up little mounds of sand. Tell them what the camels and people do at such times. Tell them where the largest desert is. Speak of the ostrich, and show picture.

SPRING, RIVER, LAKE.—Slope the sand towards one end; make a large depression in one part of it. In the highest part place a cup or bowl of water at a distance from the depression; place a few small stones in the path between the bowl and depression. Tip the bowl, allowing the water to run out slowly, but fast enough to make for itself a channel; let the children notice how it runs, changing its course when any obstruction is in the way, and filling up the depression, which will answer for the lake. Tell them the bowl is the spring; if convenient have two springs, and arrange so the streams will flow together. Speak about a real spring; ask where the water comes from, and what it makes. When several streams flow together, what do they make? Let them tell how the lake was made. Give the name of the stream that flows into the lake, also the name given to one that flows out of the lake. Speak of the river, its banks, bed, uses, etc.

Islands, Peninsulas, Capes.—Place a large piece of looking-glass on the moulding-board; let the sand run down on it for peninsulas; make several points for capes; place little piles of sand on the glass for islands. Question to bring out the right answers. Speak of coral islands; have a piece of coral to show.

Seas, Gulfs, Bays.—Arrange the peninsulas so the glass will extend into the land. Lead the children to see that the water of seas, gulfs and bays is always salt, as it is really part of the ocean.

Isthmuses, Straits.—Make the peninsulas so as to form isthmuses, and arrange the islands to form straits. Speak of canals, and make them through the isthmuses.

When all the definitions have been given, let the children arrange what the teacher calls for, the class deciding whether it is right; or let the children make anything they choose, and the class tell what they have made, and give definitions.

VILLAGE, CITY.—Use toy houses and trees to represent a village; ribbon or tape may be used for a river; a bridge of blocks may be built over it. A pleasant conversation may follow about a village. Let them tell the difference between a village and city, and convert the village into a city by placing the houses close together, making sidewalks, railroads, etc.

MEADOWS.—Green tissue paper may represent grass; horses, cattle and sheep may be placed on it; a tree here and there; a wooden or stone fence built around it—sticks stuck in, crossing each other, will do nicely. Let the children tell and do all they can, the teacher simply filling up and rounding out.

Particular parts of the earth may be represented.

COLD REGIONS.—Cotton may be laid down for snow, and piled up for icebergs. Esquimaux huts may be built of blocks, and covered with cotton for snow, or, in winter, use snow. Pictures of the people and animals may be shown and talked about. Encourage the children to make inquiries and find out all they can for themselves.

EXERCISES WITH FLAGS IN TEACHING GEOGRAPHY.

The children may be furnished with small flags of all nations. These may be purchased in paper sheets at the stationer's for a small sum. They may be cut out and to make them more durable, may be pasted on muslin and sewed to small sticks, which come in bundles.

First speak of flags generally, the significance of plain colors, their being used as signs; the white flag as the token of peace or safety; red, war or danger; yellow, sickness, etc. Ask if any have ever seen these colors used, and where.

Let the children find the flag of their own country; have them describe it; ask what colors they see; speak of the meaning of the colors: red, love; white, purity; blue, truth. Ask how many stripes it has; why thirteen; how many are white, how many are red. Have them count the number of stars; ask how many the large flags have; if convenient, have a large one to show. Ask what the stars represent, and how many the first flags had; why we have more now. Give a short history of the flag, to arouse patriotism.

Speak of the significance of the flags of different countries; how they should be treated; when they are raised; when at half-mast; why used on vessels.

Have a map of the world before the class; have

the countries pointed out; speak of the people, climate, productions, animals, etc. Name some of the most prominent mountains, rivers, cities, etc.

Taking one country for a lesson, the principal points may be written on the board, then copied and learned by the children, and reproduced on their slates the following day.

First take the countries the children know the most about, and will be likely to be most interested in. Give a country, or let them choose one to find out about for the succeeding lesson.

For review, ask for a certain flag, and have all hold it up, one or more point out the country, and each one tell some fact concerning it; also have each one present a different flag, and tell all he can about the country. Geography will thus be made a most enjoyable study, while the children will gather and retain much more knowledge than from books.

The children may pretend they live in certain countries, and tell why they like or dislike it; how they need to dress; if they are farmers, what they are cultivating; if merchants, what they are buying and selling; always making the peculiarities of the countries prominent. They may also pretend they are on board of a ship under a certain flag; they may tell of what their cargo consists, where they are going, in what direction and through what waters, what their return cargo will be, etc.

Great variety is thus attained, while interest and delight must necessarily follow.

Have the children hunt up as much as possible for themselves; ways may be suggested, books consulted and friends asked. The effort made to get the information will make it lasting. If the desire for knowledge be implanted, the teacher is doing a successful work.

For still further variety, the teacher may give the peculiarities, and the children guess the country and raise the flag. The teacher may tell a story, taking an imaginary trip around the world; as the country is mentioned or suggested, the children may raise the flag of the country.

When beginning to learn, so as not to confuse the children, only a few flags may be used, and others added as the lessons proceed.

EXERCISES WITH GELATINE PAPERS TO TEACH COLOR.

FOR FIRST, SECOND AND THIRD YEARS.

Provide the children with envelopes containing small pieces of blue, yellow, red, and, if procurable, green, orange and purple gelatine papers. The teacher should be supplied with a great variety of colored objects, such as worsteds, strings of beads, papers, cambrics, glass, ribbons, crayons, flowers, color-charts, etc. Numerical frames containing the primary and secondary colors, may now be obtained, which will be of great assistance.

The teacher may select a blue object and hold it up before the children; ask them to find the same color among their papers; call upon some to name it. Have them select all the blue objects from the teacher's collection, and name the different things they know that are blue. Teach the yellow and red in the same way. Have the children name the three colors, pointing to each, and give the term *primary colors*. Ask the color of the sky, buttercups, fire, etc.

Have the children place their pieces of blue and yellow papers together; hold them up so the light will shine through them, ask what color is made, and what colors produced it. Have them select all the greens, and name things of that color. In the same way, have them place their blues and reds together, also their reds and yellows. Let them give the three new colors made, and give the term *secondary colors*. Drill thoroughly on the combinations. Placing the colors together and seeing for themselves will fix the combinations in their minds.

The tertiary colors may be taught in the same way. If the secondary colors in gelatine papers cannot be obtained, glass may be used instead. Now test the children in all the colors learned; have them select an object, state the color, and whether it is primary, secondary or tertiary; if not primary, of what colors it is composed. When they cannot answer readily, allow them to refer to their papers.

The shades may be taught from the color chart.

Encourage the children to bring as many shades as they can find.

The colors of the rainbow may be nicely shown by means of a triangular glass prism. The colors may be thrown on the wall or on a piece of white muslin fastened up for the purpose. Explain to them the formation of the rainbow.

Teach the colors that harmonize by arranging worsteds or flowers together, and leading the children to decide what colors look well together.

When the children are left to themselves, they can write on their slates the colors learned and how formed. They may first copy them from the board, and afterward reproduce them from memory.

The blackboard work may be arranged thus:

Primary Colors. { Blue, Yellow, Red.

Secondary Colors. { Green—blue and yellow. Orange—yellow and red. Purple—blue and red.

Tertiary Colors. { Citrine—green and orange. Russet—orange and purple. Olive—green and purple.

Colors that harmonize. { Red and green—blue and yellow. Blue and orange—yellow and red. Yellow and purple—blue and red.

Reds. { Crimson, Carmine, Scarlet, Vermilion, Pink.

Yellows. { Citrine, Yellow, Lemon, Canary, Straw.

Blues.	Indigo, Ultramarine blue, Prussian blue, Light blue, Sky blue,	Orange.	Dark Amber, Orange, Salmon, Buff, Cream.
Greens.	Olive, Green, Emerald green, Pea green, Light green.	Purples.	Royal purple, Purple, Violet, Lilac, Lavender.
Browns.	Maroon, Brown, Russet, Snuff, Drab.	Colors of the rainbow.	Violet, Indigo, Blue, Green, Yellow, Orange, Red.

EXERCISES WITH WORSTED TO TEACH COLOR.

A few short pieces of worsted, of all colors, may be securely stitched by the machine between two narrow pieces of dark muslin, allowing the ends to be free for several inches. These may be distributed to the children.

They may select the colors the teacher calls for, or each one may select a color and tell what it is, and to what class it belongs; or one or all may select the primary colors, secondary, etc.

EXERCISES WITH FLAGS TO TEACH COLOR.

Muslin of different colors, cut in squares, and

sewed to sticks for flags, may be occasionally given to the children for variety in their color-lessons.

They may tell what color they have, and name all the things they can think of having the same color. If able to write, they may write a list of words, or frame the words in sentences; as, "Grass is green. Snow is white."

The teacher may relate a little story, naming as many colors as possible; when the colors are mentioned, the scholars having those colors may stand. Instead of mentioning the colors, the names of objects which always have certain colors may be used; as oranges, violets, grass, sky, dandelions, lilacs, fire, snow, coal, milk, sunflowers, lilies, crows, etc.

For instance: "A little girl with a dress the color of snow, a hat trimmed with the color of the sky, shoes the color of coal, walked through the grass to pick some violets and dandelions." This will keep their attention and require them to think; two very desirable objects. After a time the brightest scholars may be called upon to relate a story instead of the teacher. This will help them in language.

The colors of the rainbow may be taught and given in the flags, and when that is mentioned the seven having the colors may stand and arrange themselves in the proper order.

EXERCISES WITH SHOE-PEGS TO TEACH COLOR.

Packages of Diamond dyes, in primary and secondary colors, may be bought at the grocer's or druggist's for five cents a package. With very little trouble thousands of shoe-pegs may be dyed beautiful bright colors.

These will delight the children, and may be utilized in color lessons alone, or in combining color with number, form and designs.

They may be used with the boards mentioned in another chapter, or simply on slates or desks.

The teacher may dictate the arrangement, as so many of each color placed together, certain forms in certain colors, or the children may arrange them to suit their own fancies; being able to state when finished what they have done.

EXERCISES WITH FLAGS TO TEACH FORM AND COLOR.

Make small white muslin flags, and paste narrow strips of colored paper in all the different surface forms on them. The solid forms must be cut out of the sheets of colored paper; two or more colors may be used to represent one solid.

These flags serve nicely in review exercises in form and color.

Each scholar may stand in turn and state what form and color on his flag; as, "My flag has a blue square," or "My flag has a cube; the sides are blue and the top is red."

The children may also state whether their color is primary, secondary, or tertiary, and describe the form: as, "I have a green triangle; green is a secondary color; it is made of blue and yellow; a triangle has three sides and three angles."

To vary the exercises, the teacher may ask for all those who have blue on their flags to stand, and call for the other colors in the same way; also those who have certain forms, or all who have angles, or any particular kind of angles or faces.

EXERCISES WITH PICTURES TO TEACH LANGUAGE.

Have a quantity of small loose pictures, cut from old books and papers, and picture advertising cards. Distribute these among the children. Have each one tell what he sees in the picture and make a statement about each object; as in what position it is; if animals, what they are doing.

If the children see and tell too much, thus monopolizing the time they may be limited in their oral recitation to a certain number of sentences. Upon their slates they may write as much as the time will allow.

When far enough advanced, they may make up little stories from the pictures, and write them upon their slates. This will exercise their imaginations.

EXERCISES WITH CARDS TO TEACH LANGUAGE.

The following list of cards may be prepared and distributed to the scholars:

Cards with sentences having one or more words omitted, to be supplied by the children.

Cards containing singular and plural verbs, to be used correctly in sentences.

Cards containing a certain number of words appropriate for short stories; the leading words in stories with which the children are not familiar may be chosen. These words may also be used simply for separate sentences.

Cards containing names of qualities, as brittle, pliable, etc., for the children to define and give examples. The qualities are supposed to have been previously learned.

Cards containing names of objects which have been studied by the children, as coal, sponge, slate, etc.

These cards may be used for oral and written exercises. They will be a saving of the teacher's time in the class, be a great help in language, and prevent copying, as each one has different works.

BUSY-WORK TO AID IN READING, WRITING AND SPELLING.

Small cards containing separate words, which may be combined in sentences, may be done up in packages and distributed to the children, to be arranged by them, and then copied on their slates. Extra nouns and verbs may be placed in each package, so several different sentences may be made.

Where script is taught in the beginning, it is best to have the words written or printed in script upon the cards.

BUSY-WORK IN LANGUAGE.

TO TEACH CORRECT USE OF VERB.

The following questions may be written upon the board, which the children may copy, and be taught to answer in the affirmative, using the correct verb.

In a short time they will be able to make their own questions, the teacher simply placing the verbs upon the board.

Did you *go* out to-day?
Ans.—Yes, I *went* out to-day.
Did you *see* the girl?
Ans.—Yes, I *saw* the girl.
Did you *buy* a pencil?

BUSY-WORK IN LANGUAGE.

Did John *light* the lamp ?
Did Mary *find* her handkerchief ?
Did Albert *give* his brother a penny ?
Did Samuel *leave* the room ?
Did Charles *run* to school ?
Did you *study* your lesson ?
Did Helen *fan* the baby ?
Did Mrs. Stevens *make* the dress ?
Did the cat *drink* the milk ?
Did Mr. Smith *ring* the bell ?
Did Susan *wring* the towel ?
Did the baby *cry* for the orange ?
Did Peter *hang* up his hat ?
Did Nellie *sing* the song ?
Did you *think* of me ?
Did Johnny *fall* down stairs ?
Did Andrew *throw* the ball ?
Did Margaret *write* a letter ?
Did you *forgive* your brother ?
Did Sarah *forget* her book ?
Did Amanda *sweep* the room ?
Did Kate *dry* the clothes ?
Did the dog *catch* the rabbit ?
Did you *hem* the ruffle ?
Did Daniel *draw* the picture ?
Did Mark *take* the slate ?
Did Annie *blow* the light ?
Did George *shoot* the bird ?
Did the heavy weight *sink* the ship ?
Did you *seek* the little child ?

Did Walter *rise* early?
Did the sheep *lie* down?
Did you *choose* that book?
Did your mother *sleep* well?
Did Jack *swim* across the river?
Did Austin *tear* his coat?
Did the mouse *bite* the cake?
Did the blacksmith *strike* the iron?
Did the soldiers *fight* in the war?

BUSY-WORK IN LANGUAGE.

TO TEACH CORRECT USE OF ARTICLE.

1st. The scholars may write the following words, placing *an* before each.

2d. The teacher may write a certain number of these words upon the board, which the children may copy, using *an*, and they may supply the same number of different words where *a* should be used.

3d. They may write sentences, using these words with *an* before them.

4th. When learned, they may write them from memory.

ox,	acre,	eagle,	oyster,
ax,	olive,	angle,	answer,
ant,	oven,	angel,	anchor,
urn,	oval,	altar,	icicle,
inn,	iron,	honor,	armory,
eye,	axle,	arbor,	orange,
awl,	hour,	anvil,	ostrich,

ape,	echo,	agate,	anemone,
owl,	organ,	artist,	emerald,
ark,	agent,	apple,	arsenal.

overseer,	idle boy,	American,
oil-can,	errand-boy,	Englishman,
ink-well,	apartment,	Australian,
airy room,	elephant,	Irishman,
open door,	advertisement,	African.

BUSY-WORK.
OMITTED WORDS.

The scholars may copy upon their slates the following sentences, applying the omitted words:

Iron is heavy.
Feathers are light.
The sea —— deep —— salt.
—— mountain —— high.
—— elephant —— large.
Glass —— smooth.
A grater —— rough.
Cake —— soft.
Iron —— heavy.
The sun —— bright.
Snails —— slow.
Sugar —— sweet.
Vinegar —— sour.
A knife —— sharp.
Horses —— useful.
A valley —— low.

Flowers —— beautiful.
Mucilage —— sticky.
Wool and fur —— warm.
Ice —— cold.
Thread —— spun.
Cloth —— woven.
Grass —— green.
Slates —— pencils —— brittle.
Snow —— white.
The sky —— blue.
Sponges —— porous.
Coal —— black.
Lemons —— oranges —— yellow.
Bark —— brown.
Blood —— red.
Violets —— purple.
Rubber —— whale-bone —— elastic.

BUSY-WORK.

OPPOSITES.

The following list may be copied by the children, and by the side of each column they may supply the opposite meaning of the words.

up,	down.	right,	wrong.	bother,
hot,	cold.	clear,	cloudy.	screw,
left,	etc.	light,	etc.	button,
top,		weak,		coming,
old,		just,		large,

wet, poor, white,
big, good, wrong,
tall, kind, larger,
even, hard, frigid,
boy, thick, grant,
day, solid, brave,
in, well, empty,
run, head, broad,
stand, front, bitter,
obey, floor, round,
hill, first, polite,
loud, man, hungry,
open, spring, island,
deep, winter, inside,
slow, uncle, morning,
true, niece, north,
tame, father, east,
fresh, salt, brittle, sunrise,
fresh, stale, crooked, opaque,
forward, orderly, ugly,
husband, healthy, tired,
generous, grateful, sweet,
beginning, public, land,
country, sharp, rough,
locked, fastened, bolted,
coarse, foolish, ignorant,
civilized, northeast, northwest,
asleep, horizontal, living,
perfect, stupid, nothing,

BUSY-WORK.

COMPARISONS.

As shy as a fox.
As strong as a lion.
As mischievous as a monkey.
As cunning as a kitten.
As busy as a bee.
As black as a crow.
As swift as an eagle.
As stubborn as a mule.
As blind as a bat.
As slow as a snail.
As light as a feather.
As quick as a flash.
As lively as a cricket.
As heavy as lead.
As high as a mountain.
As low as a valley.
As smooth as glass.
As rough as a grater.
As green as grass.
As white as snow.
As black as ink.
As red as blood.
As blue as the sky.
As hard as iron.
As soft as silk.
As sharp as a razor.
As clear as crystal.
As sweet as honey.

As sour as vinegar.
As bitter as gall.
As light as day.
As dark as night.
As timid as a hare.
As tough as an ox.
As good as gold.
As innocent as a lamb.

The teacher may place a few of these sentences on the board at a time, and talk with the children about them. When they are familiar with them, the quality or object may be erased, and the children, copying the sentences upon their slates, may supply the omitted words.

BUSY-WORK.

DEFINITIONS.

One who teaches is called a teacher.
" preaches " " ———
" talks " " etc.
" paints " "
" writes " "
" plays " "
" reads " "
" builds " "
" works " "
" thinks " "
" sews " "
" sows " "
" farms " "

One who idles is called an
"   laughs   "   a
"   digs   "   "
"   learns   "   "
"   loves   "   "
"   tattles   "   "
"   fights   "   "
"   gives   "   "
"   runs   "   "
"   hunts   "   "
"   swims   "   "
"   prints   "   "
"   sings   "   "
"   spins   "   "
"   weaves   "   "

BUSY-WORK.

PREFERENCES.

What color   do you like best?
"   fruit   "   "
"   vegetable   "   "
"   meat   "   "
"   play   "   "
"   flower   "   "
"   berry   "   "
"   season   "   "
"   holiday   "   "
"   drink   "   "
"   story-book   "   "
"   day of the week do you like best?

What month	do you like best?	
" animal	"	"
" bird	"	"
" work	"	"
" study	"	"
" insect	"	"
" mineral	"	"
" kind of pie	"	"
" kind of cake	"	"
" kind of nuts	"	"
" kind of fish	"	"

BUSY-WORK.

DRAWING.

Cards of different shapes, small box covers, blocks, wooden forms, and similar objects may be given to the children. They may place them on their slates, hold them firmly, and draw lines around them with a sharp pencil, as smoothly as possible. This may be difficult at first, for small children, and probably may require much practice. They may fill their slates full. Each time they may have a different form.

After a while they may combine the forms to make crude designs. The teacher may give them the idea on the board, after which they may use their own ingenuity.

When they can use these simple forms nicely, shapes of leaves, flowers, fruit, simple objects, and portions of simple designs, such as are used in wall paper and carpets, may be cut out and used in the same way. Care must be taken to cut the edges very smoothly.

The children may be allowed paper and pencils when their work warrants it. This is a step towards designing, and makes a very pleasant occupation.

BUSY-WORK.

DRAWING AND COLORING.

Designs may be drawn on the board by the teacher, and colored with crayons. These may be copied by the children, at first upon their slates, and when done sufficiently well, they may be furnished with paper and colored crayons.

The children may be taught to make designs themselves; a great variety of pretty ones may be made with the square and circle. In coloring, they may use their own taste, but should be taught to select colors which harmonize.

Leaves, flowers, trees, fences, and a great variety of objects may be drawn and colored—the coloring adding greatly to the children's pleasure, and keeping them busily and happily employed a long time.

Books with pictures for coloring may be given to the very best, and when very expert, a box of paints may be added. This will stimulate them in their work.

BUSY-WORK.

QUESTIONS.

Let the pupils write the answers to these questions upon their slates.

What is your name ?
How old are you ?
Where do you live ?
Where were you born ?
How many brothers have you ?
How many sisters have you ?
What is your father's first name ?
What is your mother's first name ?
What school do you attend ?
What is your teacher's name ?
What do you study ?
What study do you like best ?
What do you do at home ?
In what country do you live ?
In what State do you live ?
In what city or town do you live ?
In what county do you live ?

OCCUPATIONS.

EXERCISES WITH CARD-BOARD, PAPER, ETC.

With pieces of card or perforated board, cut in strips, and wooden tooth-picks, many objects may be formed. The card-board may be pricked with pins to admit the ends of the sticks.

Fences and gates may be very easily made; and the children may be allowed to use their own ingenuity.

Soaked peas may be used with the sticks, with which a still greater variety of objects may be made; as air castles, furniture, houses, fences, etc. In kindergarten materials may be found cubes of cork and wires for this purpose.

Boxes.—Pieces of card-board may be converted into boxes by pasting them together with slips of paper. When they are nicely made, fancy pictures may be pasted on them, and they may be retained in school or the children may be allowed to give them away.

Paper-Folding.—Small squares of paper may be furnished to the children, with which they may be taught to make boats, soldier-caps, pin-wheels, cornucopia, and many other objects. With slips of paper they may be taught to make lamp-lighters. Newspapers may be used to practice upon, and afterward colored paper may be given.

The best work should be retained for a while, at least, and placed where it can be seen daily by the class.

Boxes may be ornamented with some of the designs, and flags may be made with them also.

ENVELOPES.—The shapes of envelopes, of different sizes, may be drawn upon card-board and cut out. These, with light brown paper, may be given to the older children. They may mark the forms of the envelopes, cut them out, fold, and, with mucilage or gum tragacanth, paste them. These envelopes may be used to practice addressing letters.

PUZZLES.—Stars, crosses, squares, circles, oblongs, leaves, etc., may be drawn on card-board and cut in various ways to form puzzles. These may be placed in little boxes, bags, or envelopes, with the names of the designs upon them. The children will enjoy puzzling them out.

Pictures may be pasted on card-board, and cut and used in the same way.

PARCELS.—Pieces of paper and small articles, such as blocks, shoe-pegs, slats, tooth-picks, and button-moulds, may be given to the children. With these they may be taught to do up neat little parcels and tie them with cord.

STRINGING STRAWS, ETC.—Squares of colored paper and short pieces of colored straw may be strung together; the children should be taught to place the needle in the middle of each paper.

Button-moulds may be colored and strung, also beads. The teacher may select the order in which the colors are to be used.

PASTING.—A chain of rings may be made by pasting together short slips of colored paper. These chains make very pretty decorations when festooned from the chandeliers or hung on the walls. At Christmas time they may be used, with pretty effect, upon Christmas trees.

SLAT-WEAVING.

Bundles of slats may be distributed among the scholars. The children may be taught to weave them in many ways. At first, designs may be drawn upon the board for the children to copy.

Picture-frames and fancy baskets may also be made.

The slats may be dyed,* and then woven in different patterns similar to the paper weaving. It would be well to begin with the slat weaving first.

EXERCISES WITH SCRAP-BOOKS.

Old copy books may be saved and given to the children for scrap-books to paste pictures in. The pictures may be furnished by both the children and teacher. Where the pictures are sufficiently light they may be colored with crayons or paints.

Narrow pieces of colored paper may be pasted around the pictures for frames. The narrow strips

---

* The diamond dyes, used for coloring eggs, may be used with little trouble and expense.

of paper may be pasted in various forms—as fences, chairs, houses, windows, benches and boxes.

Muslin scrap-books may be made by the children, the edges may be worked in button-hole stitch, with colored yarn or worsted to keep them from fraying. Sometimes covers of sample books from dry-goods stores may be obtained, which answer nicely for binding.

EXERCISES IN SEWING.

Writing paper or stiff brown paper may be folded and run through the sewing-machine (not sewed) in many different ways. It may then be unfolded and sewed, backstitch, with colored crewels or worsted, by the children. Regular designs may also be made with the machine.

Outlines of a variety of objects, as chairs, stools, tables, tools, leaves, flowers, insects, birds, animals, letters and numbers, may be drawn on cards or card-board. These may be pricked by the children, with large pins, at short distances apart for sewing. Cards already drawn, with the places marked for pricking, may be purchased where kindergarten materials are sold.

As the cards are finished they may be laid aside, and occasionally be distributed to the class, to be used as language or object lessons.

Coarse card-board may be used and served in an

endless variety of ways and designs. These exercises will help little children very much in becoming accurate in their observation and work.

They may at first begin with simple marks, then crosses, and very gradually take more difficult figures.

It is well to teach the children to make the alphabet in cross-stitch, as the knowledge may be utilized in marking towels and clothing.

Where the class is very large a portion may work at a time, a monitor may be appointed to thread needles, if necessary, and attend to the work.

EXERCISES WITH PAPER IN MAKING FLOWERS.

The children may be taught to fold slips of tissue paper and cut in the shape of flower-leaves. In making roses, three sizes of leaves should be used. The leaves may be unfolded and the larger ones moulded in the palm of the hand, with the thumb; the edges may be slightly rolled with a shawl pin.

A small common porcelain button may be fastened to the end of a small short wire. A hole may be pricked in the middle of each leaf with the pin.

Put the wire through the holes of the smallest leaves first, and fold around the button. The outer leaves need not be folded down, but allowed to lie loosely, like an open flower.

A little wax may be placed at the base of the outer leaves to fasten them securely to the wire.

These paper flowers look pretty bunched together and placed over pictures in the school-room, or arranged in little baskets and hung up.

White, red, pink, and yellow tissue paper are the prettiest colors to use.

Quite small children may be taught to make the flowers. It is very pretty work in the family.

SLATE WORK.

Names of web-footed birds.
" scratchers.
" birds of prey.
" runners.
" waders.
" cud-chewers.
" hoofed animals.
" fur-bearing animals.
" nocturnal animals.
" horned animals.
" flesh eaters.
" grain eaters.
" common animals.
" wild animals.
" insects.
" young of animals.
" houses of animals.
" relations.
" holidays.

Names of fall flowers.
" berries.
" nuts.
" meats.
" grains.
" groceries.
" fancy articles.
" dry-goods.
" spring vegetables.
" summer vegetables.
" fall vegetables.
" seeds used for food.
" roots used for food.
" stems used for food.
" leaves used for food.
" trees used for building.
" minerals.
" garments.
" stores,
" things in the room.
" things in the street.
" parts of the body.
" parts of the house.
" furniture.
" thing made of gold.
" " " of leather.
" " " marble.
" " " wood.
" " " brick.
" " " stone.
" " " clay.

Names of thing made of straw.
" " " paste-board.

A lesson may be made of each of these subjects.

SLATE WORK.

MISCELLANEOUS.

Name 3 things the door has.
Name 3 things the chair has.
Name 5 things the room has.
Name 4 things the book has.
Name 3 things the table has.
Name 4 things the cat can do.
Name 4 things the horse can do.
Name 4 things the dog can do.
Name 3 qualities of glass.
Name 3 qualities of writing paper.
Name 3 qualities of slate.
Name the parts of a coat.
Name the parts of shoes.
Name the parts of a hat.
Name the parts of a clock.
Name the objects in the room made of mineral substances.
Of vegetable substances.
Of animal substances.
Name 3 things on which you can write.
Name 3 things with which you can write.
Name 3 things in which you can ride.
Name 3 things on which you can ride.
Name things without life that have 4 legs.

Name something with 3 legs.
Name things without life that have mouths.
Name things without life that have heads.
Name things without life that have arms.
Name things without life that have feet.
Write 5 things that you can see.
Write 3 things that you can hear.
Write 3 things that you can feel.
Write 3 things that you can taste.
Write 5 things that you can do.
Write the days of the week.
Write the months of the year.
Write the colors.
Write boys' names.
Write girls' names.
Write names of streets.
Write your full name.
Write your initials.
Write your father's initials.
Write your mother's initials.
Write the initials of your State.
Draw the outlines of an envelope and write your address upon it.
Name something wrong.
Name something right.

EXERCISES WITH OBJECTS TO TEACH THE KINGDOMS.

Each child may have a box or bag containing several things from each kingdom—as stones, nuts, wire, wood, marbles, fur, sponge, wool, cotton,

EXERCISES WITH OBJECTS. 105

horse-hair, seeds, etc. These articles may be largely, if not entirely, supplied by the children. They may be allowed to have their names written upon their boxes or bags, which will give them a sense of ownership, and will encourage them to get a nice and varied collection.

The teacher may tell them to open their boxes or bags and take out something that did not grow. If they make mistakes, question them closely until they find they are wrong. This will lead them to think. Let each one hold up and name very quickly what he has taken out, stating that it did not grow.

Next, have them take out something that grew, whether vegetable or animal. Lead them to see that things that grow have life. " Things that do not grow are called minerals, or mineral substances; that of which a thing is made is called its substance." Question them as to the things they have selected that grow, whether they came from plants or animals. "Things that come from plants are called vegetable substances. Things that come from animals are called animal substances." What can the animal do which the vegetable cannot? When the animal wants things, what can he do? Can the vegetable or plant move of itself?

When they understand the three kingdoms, the teacher may ask for objects belonging to any one, and have them select; or have them select any article and tell where it belongs.

When left to amuse themselves, they may arrange their objects in groups, placing all the mineral substances together, the vegetable, etc.

EXERCISES WITH OBJECTS TO TEACH THE TERMS, NATURAL AND MANUFACTURED.

The objects may now be classified in a different way. Let them show you something that God made. Then something that man made. Lead them to see that God uses man to help make things. "Things that God made are called natural. Things that man made are said to be manufactured." They may arrange their objects according to these classes.

They may now make their selections, telling to what kingdom they belong, and whether they are natural or manufactured.

They may be continually adding to their collections, and have daily lessons upon particular objects, until they gain a knowledge of all the common things around them.

Lessons upon qualities may follow, the teacher supplying any needed articles.

EXERCISES WITH OCCUPATION CARDS* TO TEACH LANGUAGE AND NUMBER.

These cards contain on one side the parts of speech, in print and script; on the other, simple examples in the four rules. Each part of speech is printed on a different colored card. There is also a set of alphabet cards.

These cards may be distributed to the class and used in a great variety of ways. The smallest children may simply write the word that is on their card upon their slates; the older ones may write a sentence containing the word; if the word begin with a capital letter, they must place it at the beginning of the sentence; they may also copy the examples printed on the opposite side, and supply the answers.

They may write a certain number of statements containing the word, and the same number of questions; or questions and answers alternately.

When the words are names of animals, they may tell what they can do, what they eat, where they live, whether good for food, name of the food, name of their young, kind of covering, kind of feet, kind of teeth, uses to man, etc.

When names of objects, they may tell all they

* Pub. by F. F. Whittier, Farmington, Maine. Price, $1.00.

know about them; of what materials made, of what use, when and where used, their parts or shapes of parts.

If capable they may write a little story about the animal or object.

When the cards contain verbs, they may write the different forms of the verb, or sentences using the different forms. They may name the different people or animals that perform the action.

When the words are adjectives, they may name all the things to which they may be applied.

The cards may be distributed miscellaneously; several may be given to each child.

Nouns.—The teacher may ask those to raise their hands, or stand, who have names of persons, animals, birds, parts of body, things to eat, things to use, things that grow out of the earth, animals with two legs, with four legs, relations, things to wear, to live in, and articles used in the house.

Verbs.—Things that people do, that animals do, that people and animals both do.

Adjectives.—Names that show size, color, quantity, quality or kind, length, number.

Pronouns.—Words that stand for people, for objects, for boys and men, for girls and women, for both, used in asking questions, in speaking of oneself, of another, of one, of more than one.

Adverbs.—Words that tell time, ask questions, answer questions, show quantity.

Conjunctions.—Words that connect other words,

PREPOSITIONS.—Words that show relation.

NUMBER SIDE OF CARDS.—The children may stand and read the examples with the answers, or form them into practical examples.

ALPHABET CARDS may be used to spell out words. or to print upon their slates. Spaces may be ruled on their slates for the height of the letters. They may be encouraged to take great pains to make them accurately. They will enjoy printing their own names in large letters.

Where it is not convenient to buy the cards, they may be made, or the words may be written upon the board and numbered, the children taking the numbers according to their seats, and placing their own word on the top of the slate, underlining it.

The Best Educational Periodicals.

THE SCHOOL JOURNAL

is published weekly at $2.50 a year and is in its 25th year. It is the oldest, best known and widest circulated educational weekly in the U. S. THE JOURNAL is filled with *ideas* that will surely advance the teachers' conception of education. The best brain work on the work of professional teaching is found in it—not theoretical essays, nor pieces scissored out of other journals. The Monthly School Board issue is a symposium of most interesting material relating to new buildings, heating, and ventilation, school law, etc., etc.

THE PRIMARY SCHOOL

is published monthly from September to June at $1.00 a year. It is the ideal paper for primary teachers, being devoted almost exclusively to original primary methods and devices. Several entirely new features this year of great value.

THE TEACHERS' INSTITUTE

is published monthly, at $1.00 a year. It is edited in the same spirit and from the same standpoint as THE JOURNAL, and has ever since it was started in 1878 been the *most popular educational monthly published*, circulating in every state. It is finely printed and crowded with illustrations made specially for it. Every study taught by the teacher is covered in each issue. The large chart supplements with each issue are very popular.

EDUCATIONAL FOUNDATIONS.

This is *not* a paper, but a series of small monthly volumes, $1.00 a year, that bear on Professional Teaching. It is useful for those who want to study the foundations of education; for Normal Schools, Training Classes, Teachers' Institutes and individual teachers. If you desire to teach professionally you will want it. Handsome paper covers, 64 pp. each month. The History, Science, Methods, and Civics of education are discussed each month, and it also contains all of the N. Y. State Examination Questions and Answers.

OUR TIMES

gives a *resumé* of the important news of the month—not the murders, the scandals, etc., but the *news* that bears upon the progress of the world and specially written for the school room. It is the brightest and best edited paper of current events published, and so cheap that it can be afforded by every pupil. 30 cents a year. Club rates, 25 cents.

⁂ Select the paper suited to your needs and send for a free sample. Samples of all the papers (40 cents worth) for 20 cents.

E.L. KELLOGG & CO., New York and Chicago.

PARKER'S

Talks on Pedagogics.

BY

Col. Francis W. Parker,

of the Cook County Normal School.

Col. Parker needs no introduction to the teachers of America. The thousands who have drawn aid and inspriation from the *Talks on Teaching* and all to whom the name of Col. Parker has for years stood for aggressive leadership in education will want this book, which contains the results of the author's most mature thought and work.

The book is the most mature expression of the educational belief of its author, formed after many years of study and investigation.

The ideas presented and the methods outlined are the outcome of work done in the Cook Co. Normal School. The doctrine of concentration alone is of sufficient importance and interest to arrest the attention of every thinking teacher in America.

WHAT IT CONTAINS:

The following titles of the chapters of the book will indicate the subjects of which it treats: Chap. I. The Child; Chap. II. The Central Subjects of Study; Chap. III. Form as a Mode of Judgment; Chap. IV. Number and its Relation to the Central Subjects; Chap. V. What can be done with numbers; Chap. VI. Attention; Chap. VII. Observation; Chap. VIII. Language and Hearing Language; Chap. IX. Reading and its Relations to the Central Subject; Chap. X. Modes of Expression; Chap. XI. Unity of Expressive Acts; Chap. XII. Acquisition of the Forms of Thought Expression; Chap. XIII. Speech and Writing; Chap. XIV. School Government and Moral Training; Chap. XV. Summary of the Doctrine of Concentration; Chap. XVI. Democracy and Education.

The whole makes a large volume of 507 pages. Nearly two solid years have been spent in its preparation. Nearly 2000 advance orders have been received for it. It is finely printed and durably bound as a book of its value and importance deserves to be. There are topic headings and questions for the student.

Price, $1.50; to teachers, $1.20; postage, 14 cents.

E. L. KELLOGG & CO., New York and Chicago.

SEND ALL ORDERS TO
E. L. KELLOGG & CO., NEW YORK & CHICAGO. 9

Browning's Educational Theories.

By OSCAR BROWNING, M.A., of King's College, Cambridge, Eng. No. 8 of *Reading Circle Library Series.* Cloth, 16mo, 237 pp. Price, 50 cents; *to teachers,* 40 cents; by mail, 5 cents extra.

This work has been before the public some time, and for a general sketch of the History of Education it has no superior. Our edition contains several new features, making it specially valuable as a text-book for Normal Schools, Teachers' Classes, Reading Circles, Teachers' Institutes, etc., as well as the student of education. These new features are: (1) Side-heads giving the subject of each paragraph; (2) each chapter is followed by an analysis; (3) a very full *new* index; (4) also an appendix on "Froebel," and the "American Common School."

OUTLINE OF CONTENTS.

I. Education among the Greeks—Music and Gymnastic Theories of Plato and Aristotle; II. Roman Education—Oratory; III. Humanistic Education; IV. The Realists—Ratich and Comenius; V. The Naturalists—Rabelais and Montaigne; VI. English Humorists and Realists—Roger Ascham and John Milton; VII. Locke; VIII. Jesuits and Jansenists; IX. Rousseau; X. Pestalozzi; XI. Kant, Fichte, and Herbart; XII. The English Public School; XIII. Froebel; XIV. The American Common School.

PRESS NOTICES.

Ed. Courant.—"This edition surpasses others in its adaptability to general use."

Col. School Journal.—"Can be used as a text-book in the History of Education."

Pa. Ed. News.—"A volume that can be used as a text-book on the History of Education."

School Education, Minn.—"Beginning with the Greeks, the author presents a brief but clear outline of the leading educational theories down to the present time."

Ed. Review, Can.—"A book like this. introducing the teacher to the great minds that have worked in the same field, cannot but be a powerful stimulus to him in his work."

SEND ALL ORDERS TO
E. L. KELLOGG & CO., NEW YORK & CHICAGO.

Augsburg's Easy Things to Draw.

By D. R. AUGSBURG, Supt. Drawing at Salt Lake City, Utah. Quarto, durable and elegant cardboard cover, 80 pp., with 31 pages of plates, containing over 200 different figures. Price, 30 cents; *to teachers*, 24 cents; by mail, 4 cents extra.

This book is not designed to present a system of drawing. It is a collection of drawings made in the simplest possible way, and so constructed that any one may reproduce them. Its design is to furnish a hand-book containing drawings as would be needed for the school-room for object lessons, drawing lessons, busy work. This collection may be used in connection with any system of drawing, as it contains examples suitable for practice. It may also be used alone, as a means of learning the art of drawing. As will be seen from the above the idea of this book is new and novel. Those who have seen it are delighted with it as it so exactly fills a want. An index enables the teacher to refer instantly to a simple drawing of a cat, dog, lion, coffee-berry, etc. Our list of Blackboard Stencils is in the same line.

Augsburg's Easy Drawings for the Geo-

GRAPHY CLASS. By D. R. AUGSBURG, B. P., author of "Easy Things to Draw." Contains 40 large plates, each containing from 4 to 60 separate drawings. 96 pp., quarto cardboard cover. Price 50 cents; *to teachers*, 40 cents; by mail 5 cents extra.

In this volume is the same excellent work that was noted in Mr. Augsburg's "Easy Things to Draw." He does not here seek to present a system of drawing, but to give a collection of drawings made in the simplest possible way, and so constructed that any one may reproduce them. Leading educators believe that drawing has not occupied the position in the school course heretofore that it ought to have occupied: that it is the most effectual means of presenting facts, especially in the sciences. The author has used it in this book to illustrate geography, giving drawings of plants, animals, and natural features, and calling attention to steps in drawing. The idea is a novel one, and it is believed that the practical manner in which the subject is treated will make the book a popular one in the school-room. Each plate is placed opposite a lesson that may be used in connection. An index brings the plates instantly to the eye.

SEND ALL ORDERS TO
E. L. KELLOGG & CO., NEW YORK & CHICAGO. 11

Currie's Early Education.

"The Principles and Practice of Early and Infant School Education." By JAMES CURRIE, A. M., Prin. Church of Scotland Training College, Edinburgh. Author of "Common School Education," etc. With an introduction by Clarence E. Meleney, A. M., Supt. Schools, Paterson, N. J. Bound in blue cloth, gold, 16mo, 290 pp. Price, $1.25 ; *to teachers,* $1.00 ; by mail, 8 cents extra.

WHY THIS BOOK IS VALUABLE.

1. Pestalozzi gave New England its educational supremacy.
The Pestalozzian wave struck this country more than forty years ago, and produced a mighty shock. It set New England to thinking. Horace Mann became eloquent to help on the change, and went up and down Massachusetts, urging in earnest tones the change proposed by the Swiss educator. What gave New England its educational supremacy was its reception of Pestalozzi's doctrines. Page, Philbrick, Barnard were all his disciples.

2. It is the work of one of the best expounders of Pestalozzi.
Forty years ago there was an upheaval in education. Pestalozzi's words were acting like yeast upon educators; thousands had been to visit his schools at Yverdun, and on their return to their own lands had reported the wonderful scenes they had witnessed. Rev. James Currie comprehended the movement, and sought to introduce it. Grasping the ideas of this great teacher, he spread them in Scotland; but that country was not elastic and receptive. Still, Mr. Currie's presentation of them wrought a great change, and he is to be reckoned as the most powerful exponent of the new ideas in Scotland. Hence this book, which contains them, must be considered as a treasure by the educator.

3. This volume is really a Manual of Principles of Teaching.
It exhibits enough of the principles to make the teacher intelligent in her practice. Most manuals give details, but no foundation principles. The first part lays a psychological basis—the only one there is for the teacher; and this is done in a simple and concise way. He declares emphatically that teaching cannot be learned empirically. That is, that one cannot watch a teacher and see *how* he does it, and then, imitating, claim to be a teacher. The principles must be learned.

4. It is a Manual of Practice in Teaching.

SEND ALL ORDERS TO
50   *E. L. KELLOGG & CO., NEW YORK & CHICAGO.*

Welch's Talks on Psychology Applied to

TEACHING. By A. S. WELCH, LL.D., Ex-Pres. of the Iowa Agricultural College at Ames, Iowa. Cloth, 16mo, 136 pp. Price, 50 cents; *to teachers*, 40 cents; by mail, 5 cents extra.

This little book has been written for the purpose of helping the teacher in doing more effective work in the school-room. The instructors in our schools are familiar with the branches they teach, but deficient in knowledge of the mental powers whose development they seek to promote. But no proficiency that does not include the *study of mind*, can ever qualify for the work of teaching. The teacher must comprehend fully not only the *objects* studied by the learner, but the *efforts* put forth and in studying them, the *effect* of these efforts on the faculty exerted, their *results* in the form of accurate knowledge. It is urged by eminent educators everywhere that a knowledge of the branches to be taught, and a *knowledge of the mind* to be trained thereby, are equally essential to successful teaching.

WHAT IT CONTAINS.

PART I.—Chapter 1. Mind Growth and its Helps. Chapter 2.—The Feelings. Chapter 3.—The Will and the Spontaneities. Chapter 4.—Sensation. Chapter 5.—Sense Perception, Gathering Concepts. Chapter 6.—Memory and Conception. Chapter 7.—Analysis and Abstraction. Chapter 8.—Imagination and Classification.—Chapter 9.—Judgment and Reasoning, the Thinking Faculties.

PART II.—Helps to Mind Growth. Chapter 1.—Education and the Means of Attaining it. Chapter 2.—Training of the Senses. Chapter 3.—Reading, Writing, and Spelling. Chapter 4.—Composition, Elementary Grammar, Abstract Arithmetic, etc.

** This book, as will be seen from the contents, deals with the subject differently from Dr. Jerome Allen's "Mind Studies for Young Teachers," (same price) recently published by us.

FROM THOSE WHO HAVE SEEN IT.

Co. Insp. Dearness, London, Canada.—"Here find it the most lucid and practical introduction to mental science I have ever seen."

Florida School Journal.—"Is certainly the best adapted and most desirable for the mass of teachers."

Penn. School Journal.—"Earnest teachers will appreciate it."

Danville, Ind., Teacher and Examiner.—"We feel certain this book has a mission among the primary teachers."

Iowa Normal Monthly.—"The best for the average teacher."

Prof. H. H. Seeley, Iowa State Normal School.—"I feel that you have done a very excellent thing for the teachers. Am inclined to think we will use it in some of our classes."

Science, N. Y.—"Has been written from an educational point of view."

Education, Boston.—"Aims to help the teacher in the work of the school-room."

Progressive Teacher.—"There is no better work."

Ev-Gov. Dysart, Iowa.—"My first thought was, 'What a pity it could not be in the hands of every teacher in Iowa.'"

GENERAL METHODS AND SCHOOL MANAGEMENT.

Title	Binding	List	Net	Postage
Currie's Early Education,	cl.	1.25	1.00	.08
Fitch's Art of Questioning,	paper		.15	pd
" Art of Securing Attention	paper		.15	pd.
" Lectures on Teaching,	cl.	1.25	1.00	pd.
Gladstone's Object Teaching,	paper		.15	pd.
Hughes' Mistakes in Teaching. *Best edition.*	cl.	.50	.40	.05
" Securing and Retaining Attention, *Best ed.*	cl.	.50	.40	.05
" How to Keep Order.	paper		.15	pd.
Kellogg's School Management.	cl.	.75	.60	.05
McMurry's How to Conduct the Recitation,	paper		.15	pd.
*Parker's Talks on Pedagogics.	cl.	1.50	1.20	.12
" Talks on Teaching,	cl.	1.25	1.00	.09
" Practical Teacher,	cl.	1.50	1.20	.14
*Page's Theory and Practice of Teaching,	cl.	.80	.64	.08
Patridge's Quincy Methods, illustrated,	cl.	1.75	1.40	.13
Quick's How to Train the Memory,	paper		.15	pd.
*Rein's Pedagogics,	cl.	.75	.60	.08
*Reinhart's Principles of Education,	cl.	.25	.20	.03
* " Civics in Education,	cl.	.25	.20	.03
*Rooper's Object Teaching,	cl.	.25	.20	.03
Sidgwick's Stimulus in School,	paper		.15	pd.
Shaw and Donnell's School Devices,	cl.	1.25	1.00	.10
Southwick's Quiz Manual of Teaching,	cl.	.75	.60	.05
Yonge's Practical Work in School,	paper		.15	pd.

METHODS IN SPECIAL SUBJECTS.

Title	Binding	List	Net	Postage
Augsburg's Easy Drawings for Geog. Class,	paper	.50	.40	.05
" Easy Things to Draw,	paper	.30	.24	.03
*Burnz Step by Step Primer,			.25	pd.
Calkins' How to Teach Phonics,	cl.	.50	.40	.05
Dewey's How to Teach Manners,	cl.	.50	.40	.05
Gladstone's Object Teaching,	paper		.15	pd.
Hughes' How to Keep Order,	paper		.15	pd.
*Iles' A Class in Geometry		.30	.24	.03
Johnson's Education by Doing,	cl.	.50	.40	.05
*Kellogg's How to Write Compositions	paper		15	pd.
Kellogg's Geography by Map Drawing	cl.	.50	.40	.05
*Picture Language Cards, 2 sets, each,			.30	pd.
Seeley's Grube Method of Teaching Arithmetic,	cl.	1.00	.80	.07
" Grube Idea in Teaching Arithmetic	cl.	.30	.24	.03
Smith's Rapid Practice Cards, 32 sets, each			.50	
Woodhull's Easy Experiments in Science,	cl.	.50	.40	.05

PRIMARY AND KINDERGARTEN

Title	Binding	List	Net	Postage
Calkins' How to Teach Phonics,	cl.	.50	.40	.05
Currie's Early Education,	cl.	1.25	1.00	.08
Gladstone's Object Teaching,	paper		.15	pd.
Autobiography of Froebel,	cl.	.50	.40	.05
Hoffman's Kindergarten Gifts,	paper		.15	pd.
Johnson's Education by Doing,	cl.	.50	.40	.05
*Kilburn's Manual of Elementary Teaching		1.50	1.20	.10
Parker's Talks on Teaching,	cl.	1.25	1.00	.09
Patridge's Quincy Methods,	cl.	1.75	1.40	.13
Rooper's Object Teaching,	cl.	.25	.20	.03
Seeley's Grube Method of Teaching Arithmetic,	cl.	1.00	.80	.07
" Grube Idea in Primary Arithmetic,	cl.	.30	.24	.03
*Sinclair's First Years at School,	cl.	.75	.60	.06

MANUAL TRAINING.

Butler's Argument for Manual Training,	paper		.15	pd.
*Larsson's Text-Book of Sloyd,	cl.	1.50	1.20	.15
Love's Industrial Education,	c'.	1.50	1.20	.12
*Upham's Fifty Lessons in Woodworking,	cl.	.50	.40	.05

QUESTION BOOKS FOR TEACHERS.

Analytical Question Series. Geography,	cl.	.50	.40	.05
" " " U. S. History,	cl.	.50	.40	.05
" " " Grammar,	cl.	.50	.40	.05
*Educational Foundations, bound vol. '91–'92,	paper		.60	pd.
* " " " '92–'93,	cl.		1.00	pd.
N. Y. State Examination Questons,	cl.	1.00	.80	.08
*Shaw's National Question Book Newly revised.			1.75	pd.
Southwick's Handy Helps,	cl.	1.00	.80	.08
Southwick's Quiz Manual of Teaching. Best edition.	cl.	.75	.60	.05

PHYSICAL EDUCATION and SCHOOL HYGIENE.

Groff's School Hygiene,	paper		.15	pd.

MISCELLANEOUS.

Blaikie On Self Culture,	cl.	.25	.20	.03
Fitch's Improvement in Education,	paper		.15	pd.
Gardner's Town and Country School Buildings,	cl.	2.50	2.00	.12
Lubbock's Best 100 Books,	paper		.20	pd.
Pooler's N. Y. School Law,	cl.	.30	.24	.03
Portrait of Washington,			5.00	pd.
*Walsh's Great Rulers of the World,	cl.	.50	.40	.05
Wilhelm's Student's Calendar,	paper	.30	.24	.03
Bas-Reliefs of 12 Authors, each,			1.00	pd.

SINGING AND DIALOGUE BOOKS.

*Arbor Day, How to Celebrate It,	paper	.25	pd.
Reception Day Series, 6 Nos. (Set $1.40 postpaid.) Each.	.30	.24	.03
Song Treasures.	paper	.15	pd.
*Best Primary Songs. *new*		.15	pd.
*Washington's Birthday, How to Celebrate It,	paper	.25	pd.

SCHOOL APPARATUS.

Smith's Rapid Practice Arithmetic Cards, (32 sets), Each, .50 pd.
" Standard " Manikin. (Sold by subscription.) Price on application.
" Man Wonderful " Manikin, 4.00 pd.
Standard Blackboard Stencils, 500 different nos.,
    from 5 to 50 cents each. Send for special catalogue.
" Unique " Pencil Sharpener, 1.50 .10
*Russell's Solar Lantern, 25.00 pd.
Standard Physician's Manikin. (Sold by subscription.)

☞ 100 page classified, illustrated, descriptive Catalogue of the above and many other Method Books, Teachers' Helps, sent free. 100 page Catlogue of books for teachers, of all publishers, light school apparatus, etc., sent free. Each of these contain our special teachers' prices.

E. L. KELLOGG & CO., New York & Chicago.

COMMENTS OF EDUCATORS ON PARKER'S TALKS ON PEDAGOGICS.

"It is in every respect an admirable book, replete with sound philosophy, and practical methods." —Supt. JOHN SWETT, *San Francisco.*

"I find the book slow reading since it obliges me to keep up a 'brown study.' Every page bears evidence of earnest study."
—Dr. E. E. WHITE, *Ohio.*

"I am prepared to pronounce it the greatest of Col. Parker's great works. It is a work that should be *studied* by every teacher in the country." —Supt. J. H. PHILLIPS, *Birmingham, Ala.*

"It is a work of extraordinary value."
—Prin. T. B. NOSS, *California (Pa.) Normal School.*

"A masterly exposition of the theory of concentration destined to exercise great influence over educational thought and practice of the twentieth century."
—Prin. ALBERT E. MALTBY, *Slippery Rock Normal School, Penn.*

"I have examined with great interest and profit 'Talks on Pedagogics.' It is an able plea for the professional attitude. It appeals not only to the intelligence, but also to the conscience of teachers. It treats the child reverently and recognizes the varied possibilities that are opened to him through education. The doctrine of concentration, more or less new in this country, is treated, not from the theoretical standpoint, but from the point of view of honest, patient experiment and practice. As a help to teachers it will rank among the very best of current pedagogical works."
—SAMUEL T. DUTTON, *Supt. of Schools, Brookline, Mass.*

"It is a great book and indicates the profound thought and the sublime ideal inspiring the author during the years of his study of the child and education."
—CLARENCE E. MELENEY, *Teachers College, New York City.*

"I regard Col. Parker's 'Talks on Pedagogics' as one of the very best books in my library. I always read anything from Col. Parker's pen with interest and profit. This, his latest production, is his best."
—A. W. EDSON, *Worcester, Mass.*

"Parker's 'Talks on Pedagogics' received. I like it. It is a splendid acquisition to pedagogical literature. It should be in the hands of every teacher." —Z. X. SNYDER, *Pres. State Normal School, Greeley, Col.*

"It is full of wise suggestions and interesting thoughts. No teacher can afford to leave this book unread:"
—E. A. SHELDON, *Prin. State Normal School, Oswego, N. Y.*

"There never has appeared in English a book on pedagogics more pregnant with thought more suggestive to teachers, better adapted to their wants. Every chapter, every paragraph is full of suggestion and help. The principles which underlie, rather than the so-called 'methods,' receive primary attention, though there are sufficient illustrations to suggest the manner of carrying out and enforcing a principle. No one doubts after reading this book that Herbart's 'Theory of Concentration' is thoroughly sound and entirely applicable to the training of children. As American teachers we are apt to say, 'Well, that may apply in German schools, but we cannot apply it in America.' Col. Parker has proven that 'Concentration' is a sound principle in education everywhere, and that its application in our schools is entirely feasible." —Dr. LEVI SEELEY.

Price, $1.50; to teachers, $1.20; postage, 14 cts.

E. L. KELLOGG & CO, *New York and Chicago.*

BEST BOOKS FOR TEACHERS,

Classified List under Subjects.

To aid teachers to procure the books best suited to their purpose, we give below a list of our publications classified under subjects. The division is sometimes a difficult one to make, so that we have in many cases placed the same book under several titles; for instance, Currie's Early Education appears under PRINCIPLES AND PRACTICE OF EDUCATION, and also PRIMARY EDUCATION. Recent books are starred, thus *

HISTORY OF EDUCATION, GREAT EDUCATORS, ETC.

	Retail.	Our Price to Teachers	By Mail Extra
Allen's Historic Outlines of Education, paper		.15	pd.
Autobiography of Froebel, cl.	.50	.40	.05
Browning's Aspects of Education *Best edition.* cloth	.25	.20	.03
" Educational Theories. *Best edition.* cl.	.50	.40	.05
*EDUCATIONAL FOUNDATIONS, bound vol. '91-'92, paper		.60	pd.
* " " " '92-'93, cl.		1.00	pd.
Kellogg's Life of Pestalozzi, paper		.15	pd.
Lang's Comenius, paper		.15	pd.
" Basedow, paper		.15	pd.
* " Rousseau and his "Emile" paper		.15	pd.
* " Horace Mann, paper		.15	pd.
* " Great Teachers of Four Centuries, cl.	.25	.20	.03
* " Herbart and His Outlines of the Science of Education. cl.	.25	.20	.03
Phelps' Life of David P. Page, paper		.15	pd.
Quick's Educational Reformers, *Best edition.* cl.	1.00	.80	.08
*Reinhart's History of Education, cl.	.25	.20	.03

PRINCIPLES OF EDUCATION.

	Retail.	Our Price to Teachers	By Mail Extra
Carter's Artificial Stupidity in School, paper		.15	pd.
*EDUCATIONAL FOUNDATIONS, bound vol. '91-'92, paper		.60	pd.
* " " " '92-'93, cl.		1.00	pd.
Fitch's Improvement in Teaching, paper		.15	pd.
*Hall (G. S.) Contents of Children's Minds, cl.	.25	.20	.03
Huntington's Unconscious Tuition, paper		.15	pd.
Payne's Lectures on Science and Art of Education, cl.	1.00	.80	.08
Reinhart's Principles of Education, cl.	.25	.20	.03
*Spencer's Education. *Best edition.* cl.	1.00	.80	.10
Perez's First Three Years of Childhood, cl.	1.50	1.20	.10
*Rein's Outlines of Pedagogics, cl.	.75	.60	.08
Tate's Philosophy of Education. *Best edition.* cl.	1.50	1.20	.10
*Teachers' Manual Series, 24 nos. ready, each, paper		.15	pd.

PSYCHOLOGY AND EDUCATION.

	Retail.	Our Price to Teachers	By Mail Extra
Allen's Mind Studies for Young Teachers, cl.	.50	.40	.05
Allen's Temperament in Education, cl.	.50	.40	.05
*Kellogg's Outlines of Psychology, paper	.25	.20	.03
Perez's First Three Years of Childhood. *Best edition.* cl.	1.50	1.20	.10
Rooper's Apperception, *Best edition.* cl.	.25	.20	.03
Welch's Teachers' Psychology, cl.	1.25	1.00	.10
" Talks on Psychology, cl.	.50	.40	.05

SEND ALL ORDERS TO
54 E. L. KELLOGG & CO., NEW YORK & CHICAGO.

MAPS.

These maps are made on special manilla paper, size 24x36 inches. Price, 10 cts. each. Please order by number.
501 Eastern Hemisphere.
502 Western Hemisphere.
503 Mercator's Eastern Hemisphere.
504 Mercator's Western Hemisphere.
505 North America.
506 South America.
507 Europe.
508 Asia.
509 Africa.
510 Australia.
511 British Isles.
512 Mexico.
513 Canada.
514 West Indies.

SEPARATE STATES AND TERRITORIES.

48 maps, 24x36 inches. Price, 10 cents each, as follows: Please order by number.

524 Alaska.
525 Alabama.
526 Arizona.
527 Arkansas.
528 California.
529 Colorado.
530 Conn.
531 Dakota.
532 Delaware.
533 Florida.
534 Georgia.
535 Idaho.
536 Illinois.
537 Indiana.
538 Ind. Ter.
539 Iowa.
540 Kansas.
541 Kentucky.
542 Louisiana.
543 Maine.
544 Maryland.
545 Mass.
546 Michigan.
547 Mississippi.
548 Missouri.
549 Minnesota.
550 Montana.
551 N. Hamp.
552 N. Jersey.
553 N. Mexico.
554 New York.
555 Nebraska.
556 Nevada.
557 N. Carolina.
558 Ohio.
559 Oregon.
560 Penn.
561 R. Island.
562 S. Carolina.
563 Tenn.
564 Texas.
565 Utah.
566 Vermont.
567 Virginia.
568 Wash. Ter.
569 West Virginia.
570 Wisconsin.
571 Wyoming.

GROUPS OF STATES.

Size 24x36 inches. Please order by number.
Price, 10 cents each.
515 NEW ENGLAND, comprising Me., N. H., Vt., Mass., R. I., Ct.
516 MIDDLE ATLANTIC.—N. Y., N. J., Pa., Del., Md., Va., and W. Va.
517 SOUTHERN STATES (three groups). No. I.—N. C., S. C., Ga., Fla., Ala., Miss., La., and Tex.
518 No. II.—W. Va., Va., N. C., S. C., Ga., Fla., Ala., and Miss.
519 No. III.—Ark., La., Tex., and Indian Ter.
520 CENTRAL STATES (two groups). No. I.—Minn., Wis., Mich., Ia., Ill., Ind., Ohio, Mo., and Ky.
521 No. II.—Dak. Ter., Minn., Wis., Mich., Neb., Ia., Ill., Ind., Ohio, Kan., Mo., and Ky.
522 WESTERN STATES (two groups). No. I.—Wash. Ter., Idaho, Mon. Ter., Dak. Ter., Oregon, Wyoming Ter., Neb., Cal., Nev., Utah, Col., Kan., Arizona Ter., N. Mex., Ind. Ter., and Tex.
523 No. II.—Wash. Ter., Idaho Ter., Mon. Ter., Oregon, Wyoming Ter., Cal., Nev., Utah Ter., Col., Arizona Ter., New Mex.

LARGE MAPS.

These stencils make maps as large as the largest wall maps.
572 United States, 34x56 inches. Price, 50 cents.
573 Mercator's Eastern and Western Hemisphere with Western Hemisphere repeated, 34x56. Price, 50 cents.

HISTORICAL MAPS.

Please order by number.
600 Mercator's Eastern and Western Hemispheres with the Western Hemisphere repeated, showing all the routes of the early voyagers to America and around the world. Price, 50 cents.
601 Large map of the U. S. showing territorial growth. Price, 25 cents.

FRENCH AND INDIAN WAR.

Five maps, each 24x36 in. Price, 10 cents each. Set, 50 cents.
602 Map of Va. and Pa., showing Washington's home, route taken in his journey to St. Pierre, Ft. Duquesne.
603 Map of N. Y., showing all forts on the great lakes and Lake Champlain.
604 Canada, showing all the principal places and Nova Scotia.
605 Map showing British possessions before the War.
606 Map showing British possessions after the War.

WAR OF THE REVOLUTION.

Five maps, each 24x36 in. Price, 50 cents each. 50 cents a set.
607 Boston and vicinity. N. Y. and vicinity.
608 Phila., Trenton, Valley Forge, Monmouth.
609 Burgoyne's Invasion.
610 Yorktown and Southern Battle Fields.
611 Map showing Territory of U. S. at close of the War.

WAR OF 1812.

Three maps, size 24x36 in. each. Price, 10 cents each.
612 Great Lakes and vicinity, showing battle fields.
613 Washington and vicinity.
614 New Orleans.

CIVIL WAR.

Size, 24x36 in. Price, 10 cents each. $1.00 a set.
615 U. S., showing territory seceded.
616 Washington and vicinity.
617 Richmond and vicinity.
618 Charleston Harbor.
619 Miss. River, New Orleans, etc.
620 Gettysburg Campaign.

SEND ALL ORDERS TO
E. L. KELLOGG & CO., NEW YORK & CHICAGO. 55

- 621 Sherman's March.
622 Battle Fields of Ky. and Tenn.
623 Battle Field of Va.
624 Petersburg and Appotomax.

MISCELLANEOUS.
Size, 17x22 inches. Price, singly, 5 cents each. In groups with one extra design, 25 cents.

Group One—CHILDREN.
1 In a Swing. 4 Kite Flying.
2 Jumping Rope. 5 Skating.
3 Leap Frog.

Group Two—CHILDREN.
6 Feeding Doves. 9 On a Toboggan.
7 Rolling the Hoop. 10 Where am I?
8 Blowing Soap Bubbles.

Group Three—CHILDREN.
11 Two Lillies. 14 Fast Friends.
12 Training Pussy. 15 Dance, Little
13 What Do I Care. Baby.

Group Four—CHILDREN.
16 Oh, How High! 18 "My Pony Loves
17 Naughty Tab   Sugar."
 and Dash. 19 Can I Get Them?
       20 Mud Pies.

Group Five—CHILDREN.
21 Saved From 23 Learning to
 Drowning.   Read.
22 St. Bernard Dog 24 Who Broke the
 and Boy.   Window?
       25 The Milkmaid.

Group Six—CHILDREN.
26 Wide Awake. 29 The Pet Squirrel.
27 Fast Asleep. 30 Learning to
28 Have You Been   Walk.
 Bathing?

Group Seven—ON THE SEA-SHORE.
31 Star Fish. 34 Jelly Fish.
32 Hermit Crab. 35 Red Coral.
33 Lobster.

Group Eight—PRESIDENTS.
36 Washington. 39 Lincoln.
37 Jefferson. 40 Grant.
38 Jackson.

Group Nine—POETS.
41 Whittier. 44 Bryant.
42 Longfellow. 45 Tennyson.
43 Emerson.

Group Ten—DOMESTIC ANIMALS.
46 Cow and Calf. 49 Camel.
47 Horse and Colt. 50 Reindeer.
48 Elephant and Baby.

Group Eleven—DOMESTIC ANIMALS.
51 Dog. 54 Pig.
52 Cat. 55 Goat.
53 Sheep.

Group Twelve—SMALL ANIMALS.
56 Rabbit. 59 Mouse.
57 Bat. 60 Lynx.
58 Rat.

Group Thirteen—LARGE WILD ANIMALS.
61 Polar Bear. 64 Rhinoceros.
62 Lion. 65 Hippopotamus.
63 Lioness.

Group Fourteen—ANIMALS.
66 Wolf. 69 Kangaroo.
67 Fox. 70 Donkey.
68 Hyena.

Group Fifteen—FLOWERS.
71 Wild Rose. 74 Laurel Spray.
72 Calla Lily. 75 Pear Blossom.
73 Solomon's Seal.

Group Sixteen—FLOWERS.
76 Wood Violet. 79 Morning Glories.
77 Pond Lilies. 80 Fuchsias.
78 Roses.

Group Seventeen—BIRDS.
81 Quails. 84 Stork.
82 Woodcocks. 85 Swan.
83 Eagle Flying.

Group Eighteen—OLD AND YOUNG.
86 Hen and Chick- 88 Duck and Ducklings.
 ens.
87 Goose and Gos- 89 Owl and Owlets.
 lings. 90 Bird and Young.

Group Nineteen—BUILDINGS.
91 Light-house. 94 Bird House.
92 Castle. 95 Fort.
93 Wind Mill.

Group Twenty—PATRIOTIC LIST.
96 The American 99 The American
 Flag.   Eagle.
97 Liberty Bell. 100 Goddess of Liberty.
98 U. S. Coat of Arms.

BORDERS.
101 Spiral Curves.
102 Greek Fret.
103 Triangular Combinations.
104 Greek Fret.
105 Greek Pattern Anthimion.
106 Egyptian Lotos.
107 Ivy Leaf.
108 Dog Wood.
109 Holly Leaf and Berries.
110 Holly Leaf and Berries.

ROLLS OF HONOR.
111 Script Letters, plain.
112 Script Letters, fancy.
113 Old English Letters.
114 German Text.
115 American Eagle on Shield.
116 Excelsior.

WRITING CHARTS.
117 Capitals and Small Letters.
The letters are nearly 6 in. high. Size of Stencils 9x36 in. The set contains 11 charts. Price, 50 cents a set.

PHYSIOLOGY CHARTS.
Six charts, size 24x36 in. each. Price, 10 cents each. Set 50 cents.
118 Bones. 121 Lungs.
119 Skull. 123 Liver.
120 Heart. 124 Intestines.

NATURAL HISTORY CHARTS.
Price each, 10 cents, except No. 126. Size 24x36 inches. 8 nos.

And many others. Full catalogue on application.

WHAT EACH NUMBER CONTAINS.

No. 1

Is a specially fine number. One dialogue in it, called "Work Conquers," for 11 girls and 6 boys, has been given hundreds of times, and is alone worth the price of the book. Then there are 21 other dialogues.
29 Recitations.
14 Declamations.
17 Pieces for the Primary Class.

No. 2 Contains

29 Recitations.
12 Declamations.
17 Dialogues.
24 Pieces for the Primary Class.
And for Class Exercise as follows:
The Bird's Party.
Indian Names.
Valedictory.
Washington's Birthday.
Garfield Memorial Day.
Grant   "   "
Whittier   "   "
Sigourney   "   "

No. 3 Contains

Fewer of the longer pieces and more of the shorter, as follows:
18 Declamations.
21 Recitations.
22 Dialogues.
24 Pieces for the Primary Class.
A Christmas Exercise.
Opening Piece, and
An Historical Celebration.

No. 4 Contains

Campbell Memorial Day.
Longfellow   "   "
Michael Angelo "   "
Shakespeare   "   "
Washington   "   "
Christmas Exercise.
Arbor Day   "
New Planting   "
Thanksgiving   "
Value of Knowledge Exercise.
Also 8 other Dialogues.
21 Recitations.
23 Declamations.

No. 5 Contains

Browning Memorial Day.
Autumn Exercise.
Bryant Memorial Day.
New Planting Exercise.
Christmas Exercise.
A Concert Exercise.
24 Other Dialogues.
16 Declamations, and
36 Recitations.

No. 6 Contains

Spring; a flower exercise for very young pupils.
Emerson Memorial Day.
New Year's Day Exercise.
Holmes' Memorial Day.
Fourth of July Exercise.
Shakespeare Memorial Day.
Washington's Birthday Exercise.
Also 6 other Dialogues.
6 Declamations.
41 Recitations.
15 Recitations for the Primary Class.
And 4 Songs.

Our RECEPTION DAY Series is not sold largely by booksellers, who, if they do not keep it, try to have you buy something else similar, but not so good. Therefore send direct to the publishers, by mail, the price as above, in stamps or postal notes, and your order will be filled at once. Discount for quantities.

SPECIAL OFFER.

If ordered at one time, we will send postpaid the entire 6 Nos. for $1.40. Note the reduction.

SEND ALL ORDERS TO
E. L. KELLOGG & CO., NEW YORK & CHICAGO. 53

Standard Black Board Stencils.

AIDS TO ILLUSTRATION.

The need of illustration in the work of the school-room is felt by every teacher; but lack of skill in drawing is a great obstacle. To overcome this we are manufacturing an entirely new line of blackboard stencils, by which hundreds of objects may be put on the blackboard quickly and handsomely by *any teacher however inexperienced in drawing.* Indeed it can be done by almost any pupil. Our blackboard stencils beautify the school-room and make it attractive. They give good models for drawing and writing lessons. They assist the teacher in illustrating Geography, Language, Botany, and History. No class-room is complete without these available aids.

Our standard blackboard stencils are made of tough manilla paper of great strength, made specially for us, on which the design is traced. These stencils will enable the teacher to put a handsome illustration on the blackboard in Language Lessons, Geography, Physiology, History, Botany, etc., etc., and thus attract and hold the attention of the class. These stencils can be used any number of times. Five or ten minutes will give a perfect map, or a drawing of an elephant, children playing, etc. A large and perfect map of Europe, 24x30 inches, showing all the prominent rivers, lakes, mountains and large cities can be made in eight minutes. *Each stencil can be used an indefinite number of times,* and only requires a little pulverized chalk for immediate use.

WHY THE BEST.

1. All our designs are new and of a high grade of artistic merit.
2. The animals, plants, children, birds, portraits, etc., etc., are put on paper 17x22 inches in size. The maps are usually 24x36 inches in size. No other stencils on the market compete with them in size.
3. The maps are from the recent surveys and are absolutely correct in outline.
4. Each figure and map is plainly numbered and named to correspond with the catalogue.
5. Many of these stencils are arranged in groups. Each group contains five (5) Stencils, packed in a strong envelope. This envelope gives us a secure way of sending the stencils by mail, and the buyer a neat receptacle to pack each away when through using. SOLD IN SINGLE NUMBERS as well as in groups.

TWO SAMPLES FOR TRIAL.

A simple map of South America and a design suitable for a language or drawing lesson will be mailed post paid for 10 cents. We will also send a complete catalogue.

SEND ALL ORDERS TO
E. L. KELLOGG & CO., NEW YORK & CHICAGO.

Reinhart's Outline History of Education.

With chronological Tables, Suggestions, and Test Questions. By J. A. REINHART, Ph. D. Teachers' Professional Library. 77 pp., limp cloth, 25 cents; *to teachers*, 20 cents; by mail 2 cents extra.

This is one of the little books intended to be studied in connection with THE TEACHERS' PROFESSION. The publishers, by means of these publications bring to the very doors of those teachers who lack the opportunity to attend a normal school a chance to improve in the art of teaching. "Outlines of History of Education" is what its name implies, a brief but comprehensive presentation of the main facts in educational progress. The chapters are: Introduction; Education among the Greeks; Education among the Romans; Education in the Middle Ages; the Dawn of the New Era; Education and the Reformation; Education in the Seventeenth Century; Education in the Eighteenth Century; Education in the Nineteenth Century. A thorough study of this book will be a good foundation for a more detailed study of the subject. The book is well printed from clear, large type, with topic heads and questions, and is durably bound in limp cloth.

Reinhart's Outline Principles of Education

By J. A. REINHART., Ph. D. Teachers' Professional Library. 68 pp., limp cloth, 25 cents.

To give an outline of a great subject, including nothing trivial and leaving out nothing important, is a great art. This difficult task has been successfully performed by the author of this small volume, who is an educator of long experience, and a thorough student of the science of education. The first two chapters give a general view of the subject, and the other chapters treat of the intuitive, imaginative, and logical stages of education, and the principles of moral education. This is one of the volumes intended to be studied in connection with the monthly paper, THE TEACHERS' PROFESSION. Type, printing, binding are neat and durable, and like the History by same author.

REINHART'S CIVICS IN EDUCATION,

is another little book of same price and number of pages. Ready Nov. 1891.

Reception Day. 6 Nos.

A collection of fresh and original dialogues, recitations, declamations, and short pieces for practical use in Public and Private Schools. Bound in handsome new paper cover, 160 pages each, printed on laid paper. Price, 30 cents each; to teachers, 24 cents; by mail, 3 cents extra.

The exercises in these books bear upon education; have a relation to the school-room.

1. The dialogues, recitations, and declamations gathered in this volume being fresh, short, and easy to be comprehended, are well fitted for the average scholars of our schools.

New Cover.

2. They have mainly been used by teachers for actual school exercises.

3. They cover a different ground from the speeches of Demosthenes and Cicero—which are unfitted for boys of twelve to sixteen years of age.

4. They have some practical interest for those who use them.

5. There is not a vicious sentence uttered. In some dialogue books profanity is found, or disobedience to parents encouraged, or lying laughed at. Let teachers look out for this.

6. There is something for the youngest pupils.

7. "Memorial Day Exercises" for Bryant, Garfield, Lincoln, etc., will be found.

8. Several Tree Planting exercises are included.

9. The exercises have relation to the school-room, and bear upon education.

10. An important point is the freshness of these pieces. Most of them were written expressly for this collection, and *can be found nowhere else.*

Boston Journal of Education.—"It is of practical value."
Detroit Free Press.—"Suitable for public and private schools."
Western Ed. Journal.—"A series of very good selections."

SEND ALL ORDERS TO
E. L. KELLOGG & CO., NEW YORK & CHICAGO.

Quick's Educational Reformers.

By Rev. ROBERT HERBERT QUICK, M. A., of Trinity College, Cambridge, England. Bound in plain, but elegant cloth binding. 16mo, about 350 pp. $1.00; *to teachers,* 80 cts.; by mail, 10 cts. extra.

New edition with topical headings, chronological table and other aids for systematic study in normal schools and reading-circles.

No book in the history of education has been so justly popular as this. Mr. Quick has the remarkable faculty of grasping the salient points of the work of the great educators, and restating their ideas in clear and vigorous language.

This book supplies information that is contained in no other single volume, touching the progress of education in its earliest stages after the revival of learning. It is the work of a practical teacher, who supplements his sketches of famous educationists with some well-considered observations, that deserve the attention of all who are interested in that subject. Beginning with Roger Ascham, it gives an account of the lives and schemes of most of the great thinkers and workers in the educational field, down to Herbert Spencer, with the addition of a valuable appendix of thoughts and suggestions on teaching. The list includes the names of Montaigne, Ratich, Milton, Comenius, Locke, Rousseau, Basedow. Pestalozzi. and Jacotot. In the lives and thoughts of these eminent men is presented the whole philosophy of education, as developed in the progress of modern times.

This book has been adopted by nearly every state reading-circle in the country, and purchased by thousands of teachers, and is used in many normal schools.

Contents: 1. Schools of the Jesuits; 2. Ascham, Montaigne, Ratich, Milton: 3. Comenius; 4. Locke· 5. Rousseau's Emile; 6. Basedow and the Philanthropin; 7. Pestalozzi; 8. Jacotot; 9. Herbert Spencer; 10. Thoughts and Suggestions about Teaching Children; 11. Some Remarks about Moral and Religious Education; 12. Appendix.

OUR NEW EDITION.

Be sure to get E. L. Kellogg's edition. There are other editions in the market that are not only higher in price, but very inferior in binding and typography and without the paragraph headings that are so useful. Our edition is complete with all these improvements, is beautifully printed and exquisitely bound in cloth, and the retail price is only $1.00, with discounts to teachers and reading-circles.

www.ingramcontent.com/pod-product-compliance
Lightning Source LLC
Chambersburg PA
CBHW020115170426
43199CB00009B/542